Entrepreneur®
MAGAZINE'S

startup

Start Your Own

PET-SITTING
BUSINESS

*Your Step-by-Step
Guide to Success*

Cheryl Kimball

EP
Entrepreneur
Press

Editorial Director: Jere L. Calmes
Managing Editor: Marla Markman
Cover Design: Beth Hansen-Winter
Production: Eliot House Productions

This publication is designed to provide accurate and authoritative information in regard to the subject matter covered. It is sold with the understanding that the publisher is not engaged in rendering legal, accounting or other professional services. If legal advice or other expert assistance is required, the services of a competent professional person should be sought.

Library of Congress Cataloging-in-Publication Data is available

ISBN 1-932531-06-8

Printed in Canada

11 10 09 08 07 06 05 04   10 9 8 7 6 5 4 3 2 1

Contents

Appendix

Glossary

Preface

The world is full of two kinds of people—those who can't wait to open their own business and those who would like to but are terrified by the thought.

Of course, many people fall somewhere in between: those who definitely intend to start a business but are a bit nervous about it. Perhaps that describes the point where you are.

The prospect of leaving a full-time job and its steady income can be a source of great anxiety for the would-be entrepreneur. Such a dramatic change can put anyone's nerves on edge! However, the following best practices for business start-up can alleviate a good amount of the start-up jitters. In a world where even a quick jaunt to the grocery store can be fraught with complications, the hassle and risk associated with starting your own business might seem downright foolhardy.

But you love animals and have always wanted to have a career working with them. You've also dreamed of owning your own business. The great news is that you can do both. Pet sitting is fast becoming a viable way not only to earn a living, but also to be your own boss and make a profit!

Pet sitting is a service business. Other service businesses include hair salons, dry cleaners, and auto repair or oil change shops. Restaurants fall somewhere in between service and retail, but don't worry, with pet sitting the most you will need to worry about food preparation is in dishing out a dog's kibble.

Pet sitting is also one of those businesses that does not take a huge amount of money in start-up costs. At its most basic, you can get going with some word-of-mouth advertising and reliable transportation. And if you live in a city, that transportation can be as cheap as bus or subway fare!

In a city, of course, there won't be as many pets to take care of—cities aren't hugely dog-friendly and cats can often be left to fend for themselves for a few days. However, city dogs need a lot more care than dogs that live in the country. This includes daily walks both for exercise and to relieve themselves. So a pet sitter in the city can expect to do well, but your market may need to widen to encompass more pets.

Pets in rural areas—farm dogs and barn cats—usually don't need much in the way of pet sitting. Often this is because real farm folks don't go anywhere—as the old saying goes, it takes a week to catch up from a day away from the farm! And barn cats are mostly self-fed with rats and mice.

But the suburbs, ah the suburbs are a pet sitter's dream! People in the suburbs often left the heart of the city precisely so they could have pets and a yard. These communities are teeming with people who make a good living, and can afford a pet sitter. What's more they are away a lot, gone all day to that job that pays so well. Summer vacations, business trips, and long commutes all drive up the lonely dog quotient, which is where you come in. So if you live in suburban America—pet sitting may be just the right ticket.

This book will let you in on the ups and downs of the pet sitting business. It can be relatively easy to get started. But you also need to be realistic about the idiosyncrasies of the pet sitting business. The job is demanding, both in time and in responsibility. Besides being good with animals, you must also be an excellent time manager. Last but not least, you need to have all the skills that every business owner needs to have—customer service skills, organizational skills, the ability to keep good records, the ability to collect on debts.

But the biggest thing you need to be is trustworthy. Your clients are entrusting precious members of their families to you. They need to feel confident that you will show up when you said you would, that you will take good care of their pets, and that they can entrust you with the keys to their homes and all the contents in them. That's a big responsibility!

That said, pet sitting can be one of the most rewarding businesses to run. All of the pet sitters interviewed for this book brought up one critical point: helping people take good care of their pets makes them feel very good about their jobs. How many people can say that?

1

Your Customers
Are Human

You love animals. You would love to work for yourself. Why not, you think, combine the two in some sort of animal-related business? Good idea.

There are many animal-related businesses you could start—a grooming salon, a doggy day care facility, a pet supply shop. But most of these can get expensive, for the simple reason that they require real estate. In terms of start-up costs, one of the least expensive animal-related businesses you can start is a pet sitting business.

But wait. You begin to design brochures, and you realize that there's not a pet on the planet that will be reading your brochure. You need to appeal not to the pet but to the pet's owner—who is, of course, human. It is with humans that you will be discussing the details of your service over the phone—and from whom you will be getting payment.

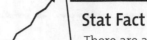

Stat Fact

There are approximately 68 million dogs and 73 millions cats in the United States today. One-quarter of all American households contain a dog and one-third of all households have a cat. For every human being born, seven puppies and kittens are born.

"It's important to be an animal lover," says Tanya K., a pet sitter in New Hampshire, "but you have to be a people person."

The service industry isn't for everyone. Providing people with a service can be frustrating at best and hair-pulling at worst! People are picky (face it, so are you—think about your own feelings when it comes to getting your hair cut, your clothes dry cleaned, or being waited on in a restaurant) and if you aren't the people-pleasing type, customers can drive you downright crazy.

Of course, while the pet owner is away, you will be fulfilling your original intent—interacting with animals. In fact, Eva and Dorothy of DEPetWatch in New York find that after their initial interaction with the pet owner, which can be somewhat involved, the lion's share of their contact is with the pets, other than the scheduling of new appointments.

A word to the wise: your marketing efforts will be directed toward humans, not animals. If that fact is OK with you, let's continue!

Where to Start?

The steps to starting a pet sitting business are the same as any other business. You will need to

- determine that there is a market for your business in your area.
- determine what you want out of your business, both financially and professionally.
- choose an organizational structure.
- choose a name.
- create a business plan.
- get financing if necessary.

- obtain the appropriate licenses and permits.
- set up your base of operations.
- create marketing materials to attract customers.

Every business needs a structure, a business plan, and a base of operations, even if that base is your car. Service businesses are often uncomplicated and start-up can be less expensive than other kinds of businesses. You often don't need a lot of stuff to get going as you do in retail. Occasionally, a service business needs some piece of specialized equipment—for instance if you were to do rug cleaning—but most everything you need for pet sitting will be supplied by the pet's owner except your mode of transportation to get you to your jobs.

We'll get to the above points in detail in other chapters throughout this book. But before you spend time and money creating a business plan and sending out brochures you must ask yourself an important question: Is there a market for a pet sitting business in your area?

Is Anybody Home?

You hope not! For pet sitting, you are looking for pet owners who are away from home at least occasionally, if not regularly.

Now that you've become fully aware that your customers are human, what group of humans in the general human population are they? And, more to the point, are these kinds of people prevalent within a reasonable market area?

Pet sitting customers do have a few common characteristics. The main one is that they are almost always gainfully employed. And there is no better customer to have in any business than one who earns a steady income! The second thing is that your customers are away from home either occasionally or often.

The two key reasons that people are looking for a pet sitter are work and vacation. Many pet sitting customers need to travel for their jobs. They make enough money at that job and have paid vacation time, which means they want to go on vacation a couple of times a year in addition to a few long weekends. Most of those instances—business travel and vacation travel—are not appropriate for pets to come along.

Many pet sitting customers are well educated—in other words, they have a

Bright Idea
Consider working for the competition before you start your own pet sitting business. Be up front about your intentions—if you are good enough, your competitor will be happy to have reliable backup when she is booked and can't take a job for a good client.

3

college education that enables them to make sufficient money to employ a pet sitter. But their education also places them squarely in the demographic of people who believe that pets are part of the family, as deserving of good care and contentment as any other family member. So when the family goes away, the pet is well cared for. More and more families are beginning to feel that their pets will be much more content if they stay in the comfort of their own home rather than go to a kennel. That's where you come in!

Laboratory Research

How do you find out if gainfully employed pet owners exist in sufficient numbers in the area you would like to designate as your market? The following are some possibilities.

- *Is there a local pet store?* If so, how busy is it? Besides simple observation, you can ask the pet store owner if he has determined a need for a pet sitting business in the area.

- *How many veterinarians does the area support?* In some areas, new veterinary hospitals are popping up every year. After you make this observation, stop at the veterinary offices some weekday afternoon (when they are least busy) and ask the staff at the front desk if they get questions from clients regarding reliable pet sitters. Veterinary offices can be your biggest allies, either through word of mouth or simply through leaving a poster on their bulletin board or, if they don't mind, a stack of business cards on their counter.

- *Are there large businesses in your area?* Are there large professional office parks with lots of white-collar businesses?

- *Check with the area chamber of commerce.* Their knowledge of business in the community can help.

Fun Fact

The American Veterinary Medical Association puts out a comprehensive book useful in researching any pet-related business venture. *The AVMA US Pet-Ownership and Demographics Sourcebook* contains chapters on "Profiles of Pet-Owning Households" and "Pet Owner Demographics." Your local library may have a copy or may be able to get you one from interlibrary loan sources. You can purchase the book from the AVMA for $99 plus $10 s/h. Their address is Division of Membership and Field Services, 1931 North Meacham Road, Suite 100, Schaumburg, IL 60173, (847) 925-8070 ext. 6683.

Cat Fight or Mutual Grooming

What if there is already a pet sitting business established in the area you would like to serve? Do you toss your idea? Hardly. Pick up the phone and ask the owner of that business if she thinks there is enough of a market to support two pet sitting businesses.

Pet sitting is a unique business venture, even among other service businesses. An extremely busy auto body shop simply schedules their customers according to their needs and constraints. In pet sitting, your schedule is dictated by your customers. If your customer calls and says he is headed for Atlanta on Friday for a four-day conference and would you look after his pets, you can't tell him you're too busy but you'll book him for the following weekend! You refer him to someone else.

When you do these kinds of referrals, you do take the risk of losing him as a customer to the referral pet sitter. However, you also may help him out enough that he remains your loyal customer—knowing he now has reliable backup if you have to say no. So a competitor is as much a referral service that can help you retain business as it is a competitor to which you may lose business.

The Odd Dog Out

You will want to think of ways to distinguish yourself from other pet sitting businesses in the area. Perhaps there are already ways in which you are different—your credentials, your experience, your personal background. Be sure to promote these unique traits in your marketing materials. If your business includes farm animals and you grew up on a thoroughbred racehorse farm in the middle of Kentucky bluegrass country, don't keep that fact hidden deep in your resume. Flaunt it on your flier and let potential customers know that you have particular expertise that the competition does not.

What Do Humans Want?

In any service-oriented business, there are key things that customers want. But when you are taking care of their pets, you need to provide these things in spades. What are they?

Trust

Pet owners will need to feel you can be trusted implicitly. This is the most critical element of a pet sitter's resume. Not only will you be taking care of their beloved pets (who they consider, by the results of several recent surveys, to be family members), but often you will be entrusted with the key to their home and access to all its contents.

There are many ways to instill this trust—your advertising, your marketing materials, and your demeanor both in person and over the phone whether it's personally or with your answering machine. Each point of contact with the public is an opportunity for you to build trust. You will certainly be expected to provide references and you should have a list of them ready at a moment's notice. Be sure to forewarn those people that you are starting a pet sitting business and that you are putting their names on your reference list. If a potential client calls, you don't want your reference to sound surprised and stammer to come up with some appropriate comments because they haven't seen you in years.

Confidence

In order to woo customers for pet sitting, you need to gain their confidence. They need to believe that not only are you trustworthy enough to be given a key to their home, but you are completely, utterly, and totally reliable. How do you do that? By being completely, utterly, and totally reliable. And then let those customers who have the utmost confidence in you spread the word! Once your business is up and running, you can begin to use your existing clients as references for potential customers.

Professionalism

As with any business, you need to look professional. That doesn't mean that your business cards can't have a picture of a fluffy little Pomeranian with a bow in her hair on it—in this business they can! But you will want to have business cards, brochures, perhaps a few ads in appropriate local newspapers, a listing in the phone book, and an answering machine or personalized answering service. All of which make you seem like you are neat, reliable, and professional. We'll cover all those print materials in Chapter 4 on marketing.

Be sure to give estimates and invoices in print and on professional stationery. Don't be loosey-goosey with your communication—if you are, a client may feel you are also going to be sloppy with getting to his house to walk his dog at the appointed hour.

Also, you need to look professional when you meet clients and potential clients in person. A professional-looking pet sitter doesn't dress in a business suit! Khakis, clean jeans, T-shirts or knit polo shirts, and sturdy walking shoes or sneakers is probably more appropriate attire. You don't want to appear looking like you will be offended if

Fifi jumps all over you and scratches your pantyhose. Or if Bob, the long-haired Burmese cat, rubs half his coat on your raw silk pants. Look like you would be willing to get down on your knees and greet the dog or crawl under the porch to reach the cat in his hiding place when the neighbor's dog chases him under there. But try not to look like you just did all those things. It's a fine line, but in general, "business casual" is appropriate attire in this business.

Reliability

When you agree to meet the client at 10:00 A.M., get there at 9:50. Always be on time, preferably even a little early. Your clients may not worry if they arrive home from work at 6 P.M. or 7:30 to get their dog out, but they care what time you arrive if they are paying you to get there at 6 P.M. to care for a pet.

Customer Care

Here are a couple of scenarios you may well have experienced yourself.

You spend your time, gas money, and a little slice of patience to get to the auto parts store. When you walk up to the counter, the clerk is on the phone with a potential customer and continues to talk for several minutes without so much as acknowledging your presence or, better still, requesting that the phone customer wait for a moment while the clerk tends to, the customer standing in front of him with your wallet out.

Or you go to a shoe store and find a pair of boots you would like to buy. But they don't have your size. The clerk happily offers to order you a pair of the boots, but you aren't sure whether you need a size 6 or 7 since there are none there for you to try on. The store clerk, however, is only willing to order one or the other size. You want to say forget it, but you really liked the boots. You tell her to order the size 7. When you go back to try them on, you feel like the size 7 is just a tad too big. But you have no point of comparison. Once again the clerk offers to order the size 6. Now you, the paying customer, will have to make your third trip to the store, which is 12 miles from your home. You, the customer, are the one doing the work here to spend your hard-earned money at this business.

Both of these scenarios are examples of where customers have been made to feel unimportant. In the first case, the customer who has made the effort to go to the store and is standing there with his wallet out should be given priority. The customer on the phone should be put on hold, even if it is just long enough to acknowledge the presence of the customer at the counter with a friendly welcome and "I'll be with you in just a minute, I'll make this call as short as possible." Better still would be to get the caller's phone number and offer to call her right back.

In the second example, the customer has indicated a willingness to buy the boots. The store should do whatever is reasonably possible to make this purchase happen—

that purchase will very likely lead to at least one other customer through word-of-mouth advertising.

While neither of these retail scenarios are ones that will come up in your service business (unless you have a retail pet supply store along with your pet sitting service), all businesses have the opportunity to make their customers feel either dispensable or important. Choose the latter every time and you will retain old customers and gain new ones.

The simplest thing you can do is the one mentioned above—return people's calls. It may be simple, but it is also one of the most important things you can do to make customers feel appreciated. Another seemingly little thing you can do is to remember your customers' pets' names (and your customers' names as well, of course!).

> ## ⚠ Beware!
> Having your business landline forwarded to your cell phone is simple to add to your phone service and can be turned on and off at will. However, if your fax line comes in through your business line, be aware that the fax calls will now come to your cell phone as well! New services are cropping up almost daily—like cell phones and landlines sharing the same phone number—so check for the latest services that make sense for you.

Giving Good Customer Service

All businesses deal with customers. Good customer service is the key to a successful business. How do you give good customer service in the pet sitting business? It all starts with the phone and ends with excellent pet care.

The steps are simple:

- *Make a good first impression.* Potential clients are probably going to contact you the first time by telephone. If you are not there to answer the phone, be sure to have a warm but businesslike personal message on your answering machine or voice-mail service. Don't use those automated telephone company-provided messages. A computer-generated voice on the other end of the line does not give the caller confidence that a business actually exists, that a message will ever get through to the right person, or that he even has the right number to begin with.

- *Be accessible.* You might think that prospective customers will consider you a busy person with a successful business if they can never get in touch with you, but in the service industry this may work against you. They may also think that you are never around, that you will be impossible to reach if they have an emergency or a question while they are away, and that perhaps you mostly spend your time on the golf course instead of working at your business.

Pet sitting may mean, that you are on the road a lot, but don't expect customers to figure out what a day in the life of a pet sitter is like. Include your cell phone number on your landline voice-mail message. If you have a pager, include that as well. Prospective clients may not bother trying to reach you via all of those methods, but they will be comforted by the impression that if they became a client and had to reach you, they could. With the portability of phone service these days, you can even have your business phone forwarded to your cell phone or wherever you might be for an extended time. Customers expect a real person to answer the phone of a small business most of the time.

- *Call people back as soon as possible.* Check your voice mail or answering machine often. In your message, ask callers to leave the best time to reach them and then call them back in that timeframe even if it means calling from your cell phone while you are away from your office. You might even be able to squeeze in a return call while today's client's Lhasa Apso is wandering around the yard looking for the best place to do his business. Don't, however, talk long while you are working. Tanya K., the New Hampshire pet sitter, chooses to shut her cell phone off when she is on a job to avoid being distracted. Just leave a message letting the prospective client know you have received her call and that you will be in touch the next morning, or the following afternoon, or, if you get a person on the phone, find out when you are both available. If the call is from a current client—not just someone you sit for occasionally, but someone for whom you are pet sitting that very day—call him back immediately.

- *Have answers to clients' and prospective clients' questions.* People will have specific questions and concerns about hiring someone to take care of their pets. Have answers to these questions. Occasionally someone will stump you with something. But if someone asks if you know how to give shots to a diabetic cat, you should have an answer. Don't say, "Well, I'm not sure." If you can and have before, say so. If you never have given shots, you can say that but also add that you are willing to learn if the pet owner would like to teach you. (If the pet owner can do it, so can you. Don't charge extra to make a visit to learn how to give the injection, consider it a useful tool that you will be able to use with other clients. Read more about this kind of thing in Chapter 5 on Credentials.)

Pest Control

Service businesses are especially prone to having a small percentage of customers who want to take up the largest percentage of your time. Your customers are the key to the financial viability of your business. That makes them necessary and a valuable component, but it also means each customer has to make you money, not cost you money. If you are spending two hours a week on the phone with Mrs. Smith discussing the details of Fluffy's bowel movements the day you took care of him or Mrs. Smith calls you back seven times to make sure you will remember to go by her house Friday afternoon to take care of Fluffy, this is time consuming. Your time needs to be compensated.

At first, you may let Mrs. Smith be a little neurotic about a new person taking care of Fluffy. But after you have proven yourself reliable and she has become confident in your services (exhibited by her willingness to use you repeatedly), you need to make sure that Mrs. Smith's business is in fact earning you money, not costing you.

There are a few ways you can deal with a client like this:

- *Take control of the conversation when she calls.* You need to be the one who determines when you will hang up. This can become a bit of an art—you don't want to hang up on her; that won't get you repeat business. But you need to make it clear that you have things to do and leave the conversation on a pleasant note.

- *Increase the fee you charge Mrs. Smith.* You can tell her your general rates have gone up or you can make sure your fee schedule explicitly charges for follow-up phone time over one 15 minute call.

- *Finally, you can be blunt with Mrs. Smith.* If you are a master of diplomacy—and you should be if you are going to start any service business—simply find a polite but firm way to tell Mrs. Smith that she takes up too much of your time with her repeated calls and that you are happy to chat with her once after your visit but more than that will require an additional charge.

There are also a couple of ways you can offset the phone calls. You should plan to leave a follow-up note with every client (see Chapter 3 on basic services for more details on this). Pet sitter Amy C. in Maine is adamant about the importance of leaving notes for owners after each pet care visit. Perhaps with Mrs. Smith, you should take a couple of minutes to leave notes that are longer than usual and see if that is enough to offset a phone call from her. If it is a big enough deal, try making her an audiotape to see if that satisfies her! You might also try considering making a follow-up call to her before she calls you. This really gives you control of the call and you are calling her on your schedule—which may not be perfect for her, so she may be quite willing to make the call a quick one because you may have caught her just before she was leaving the house for an appointment. In fact, figuring out when she may definitely be busy—perhaps, you learn that she plays bridge every Thursday evening at 7:00—and calling her a half hour before she usually leaves the house can be a very useful way to keep a call short.

Sometimes, unfortunately, it may just pay to drop a customer from your books. If the person is too much of a pain in the neck, there is also the likelihood that that same person will become annoyed with you and even increase the potential for a lawsuit. Some people cannot be satisfied. Let another pet sitter, someone new to the business who is hungry for customers, take on these kinds of clients. Some customers just aren't worth it.

Are You Ready?

Are you trustworthy, professional, and reliable? Do you instill confidence about your abilities as a pet caretaker and your interest in animals? Then keep reading, you've got a business to run!

Tip...

Smart Tip

If there are lots of hotels in your area, determine which ones allow pets. Post your fliers or leave business cards there. Guests with pets may retain your service to tend to their pet while they go sightseeing for the afternoon. You will need to have access to professional services, such as veterinary care, to enable people to feel comfortable entrusting their pet to a stranger in a strange town, but it just might be a perfect niche!

2

The Working
Parts

How you set up your pet sitting business is critical to your success. Only you know how you like to work. If you are going to work for yourself, you might as well set things up to suit you!

Many people who go into business working for themselves work from home and then set their days up just as if they were working in an office for someone else. If that is how you need to arrange your business to accommodate your customers, then that's what you should do. But pet sitting doesn't need to conform to a nine to five schedule, nor should it.

In fact, pet sitting might be more like nine *and* five. There may be no pressing business during the middle of the day, but this is no reason to sit on your hands. In a later chapter, we will explore marketing materials and advertising that you could be creating or financial information that you could be recording or analyzing but right now let's see how your business might be constructed.

Business Setup

First, there's the nasty little topic of business structure that you need to address. There are several possibilities.

- *Sole proprietorship.* This is the route that most pet sitting businesses will take. The good news about this setup is that it is simple. The business is just you— you make the decisions, and you get all the revenue. You also put up all the money and you risk all of your own personal assets. That's the bad news of sole proprietorship.

- *Partnership.* A partnership structure means that you and one or more other people are the owners/managers of the business. Dorothy and Eva, pet sitters from New York, have a partnership business. Both do it as full-time careers, and each has a full complement of customers.

- *Limited partnership.* This is where you are the main owner/manager and your partner (or partners) is a silent investor. The benefit of any type partnership is that you have someone to share everything with—the liability, the decision making, and the work. The downside of the partnership structure is that you have someone to share everything with—e.g., the revenue. So it can be harder to make money, but the theory is that two heads are better than one. The tax structure is also better with a partnership, no small consideration.

- *Corporation.* The most appealing part about the corporation structure is that the corporation becomes the entity that is at risk, not you personally. It can be a little expensive to set up a corporation, mostly because you probably want to hire a lawyer to do it. It is possible to do it yourself, but you will probably need to involve a lawyer on some level.

McPet Sitter?

The other possibility for your business structure is to consider buying into a pet sitting franchise. One of the closest analogies in service business franchising is Merry

Three Tips

1. Set aside a work area devoted to your business, even if it is just a small computer desk in the corner of the living room with a wall schedule and shelving to hold supplies. You will feel more organized when talking with potential clients and doing your bookkeeping. Your family will be happy that your business is not spread all over the house.

2. Don't procrastinate about tasks you need to keep up with, such as book-keeping. Either do a little every day so you don't get overwhelmed, or bite the bullet and hire someone to do it for you. Consider hiring your high school-aged niece to come by a couple of hours a week and keep your records up to date. She will love the gas cash or shopping mad money, and you will love having your books up to date without having to do them yourself.

3. Figure out your business hours and put your business first during those hours. For the pet sitter, you will probably find that your busiest hours are first thing in the morning and last thing in the afternoon, taking care of people's pets at the beginning and end of the day. Don't schedule appointments and activities during those times; leave them free for your business. You don't want to spend your time making doctor, dentist, and hairdresser appointments and rescheduling them because you got a job for that day. If the day arrives and you don't have a client lined up, use the time to prospect for new clients, create a new brochure, do some research, or read this week's barrage of pet- and business-related magazines.

Maids house cleaning service. This business has one main thing in common with pet sitting: People are entrusting you to come into their homes.

Certainly a key benefit of buying into a franchise is that you get immediate name recognition. But there are other benefits as well, depending on the franchise. These could include training, marketing materials, forms, start-up packets, start-up loans, and other things to make it easier to open your business.

Some disadvantages of a franchise may come in the form of control—they have it, you don't. Typically a franchise will determine where your business is located (although with pet sitting this isn't as much of an issue) and they definitely want control over how you present yourself to the public, from the advertising you use to signage to what you offer for products for sale. The parent company will also have a firm say in what your target market can be, because they will want to sell as many franchises as possible and don't want you to squeeze into another potential market. If control is a big thing for you, you would most likely be better off starting up an independent business.

Franchises can be expensive to buy into, so you really need to decide if it is worth the investment. Here are some expenses you can expect to pay:

- An initial investment fee, usually several thousand dollars
- An ongoing "royalty" fee where you pay a percentage of your sales to the parent franchise
- An advertising fee, sort of co-op advertising dollars—you pay your share of the franchisor's overall national advertising campaigns.

Smart Tip _Tip..._

Check your answering machine often for messages. You never know when a client might be desperate for a last-minute service. You don't want to miss a job just because you didn't check your messages. And if the client tries another pet sitting service to fill that emergency need, you might have just lost a client!

You should definitely investigate the franchise as carefully as possible; check their Dun & Bradstreet rating, with the Better Business Bureau for any complaints registered against the franchise, and if they have ever filed for bankruptcy or had other court-related proceedings. Retaining a lawyer to read over the fine print of the contract is probably best; you want to know up front what every possible cost will be.

If you are more the type who likes to do the work and not the type who likes to create things, then a franchise situation may work great for you.

Pet Sitting in the Clients' Homes

Taking care of your clients' pets in their homes is probably the way that most of your clients will be cared for. Studies have shown, and logic prevails, that when their humans are away, pets are more comfortable remaining in their own homes than being shuttled off to a kennel.

Pet care in the pet's home environment creates myriad things you need to be aware of. First, it will require a home visit when the owner is still at home in order to become familiar with the pet's home setup, get the grand tour, find out where the food is, where the owner allows the pet to roam in the house, and even the basics like how to get in and how to shut the alarm system off if there is one. Tanya K. in New Hampshire finds that the average initial consultation takes around an hour.

Going to the pet's home to care for her means that you will probably have to visit twice a day. This will have a great bearing on how wide a range you will accept as a market. If you have to drive twice a day to someone's house, you will want to make sure it isn't a 90-minute trip each way!

Pet-Related Things You Need to Think Of

You unlock the front door of the home where your weekend pet sitting job is. The thermostat has been set lower than it might be if the owners were home, but nonetheless it seems significantly colder than you expected it to be. What do you do?

If it's January in Vermont, your customers will probably be grateful if you call the furnace company; a house that is left a couple days without heat in a Vermont winter is probably going to have frozen, and perhaps burst, pipes when the homeowners return from their weekend away.

If it's September in Vermont, frozen pipes will unlikely be an issue. Even if it drops slightly below freezing for one night, the interior of the house will probably remain above freezing. However, even though the pipes may not freeze, the pets in the home may be in jeopardy. Birds and some reptiles and smaller animals are not able to deal with cold temperatures. Getting that furnace running again may mean the difference between life and death for the pet who has been entrusted to your care. And if the furnace is not running, there may be a malfunction that could cause carbon monoxide buildup or danger of fire, so it is best to call in a professional.

How that pet fares under your care is certainly going to have an impact on your continued relationship with that client and may have an impact on your business overall. Remember, satisfied customers tell a couple of people on average; unsatisfied customers tend to tell a couple dozen people!

Smile!

Get a digital camera and spend a little extra money to get a portable photo printer. You can use this for two great things in your business: one is to take a recent snapshot of the client's pets to attach to the client's basic information file. That way if the pet, heaven forbid, ran off, you would be able to have a picture to post or show people to help you search for the pet.

Also, pet owners love photos of their pets! The other more fun way to use the digital camera is to leave a funny picture for your client of her pet doing something cute or just looking relaxed while she was gone. This is a nice touch to include with your visit notes and will make you a memorable pet sitter.

Pet Care in Your Own Home

We will cover creating a separate kennel at your home in Chapter 12, "Expanding Your Business." But maybe you have thought you might do pet care right in your own home. The overhead would be nominal, you wouldn't have to do all that driving, and the pet would be happy because you would have more time for him, right? Well, maybe.

Like people, house pets get accustomed to their own home and their own routines. With their owner gone, their routine gets thrown out the window. Add to that a strange house, especially if you have pets of your own, and things can become a totally different deal.

The idea of pet sitting with your clients' pets in your home should be thought over very carefully. It's one thing to take care of your mother's little dog while she is in Florida for two weeks. It's quite another to incorporate a strange pet into your household.

"Most people doing this," says Amy C. of Amy's Animal Care in Maine, "are pet lovers and have too many pets of their own" to take other people's animals into their homes. "I rarely take dogs into my house," Amy says, "my dogs are just too active."

Pet Sitting as a Side Job

If pet sitting is a side job for you, a way to make extra money beyond your nine-to-five job, you may be able to expand your market, near your home and to include areas near your job. So perhaps you work an hour's commute from your home; in that case it would make sense to take on jobs an hour away from home, just not an hour in the opposite direction from your office!

Expanding your market to encompass your work area can make up some of the income you lose from the fewer clients you can take on. However, there are a couple of things to keep in mind with this sideline approach.

- Are you in a job where you might get called away on a business trip at the last minute? If so, you cannot risk being called away the same week your client is out of town. You might be able to make up for this by having a helper who can fill in for you in a pinch or take up the slack if you get more clients than you can handle with a full-time job (although if that's the case, perhaps it's time to go into pet sitting full time!). But remember, in a service business, your clients are hiring you personally as much as they are hiring a service.

- If you were to arrive at your client's house to take care of their pets before heading to work, what would happen if there were something that required you to take extra time—perhaps the pet was injured overnight or seemed sick and in need of veterinary care or at least an hour or so of observation. Is your employer and/or your type of work flexible enough for you to be able to come in a couple of hours late? What if this happened three times in one week? Would you be at risk of losing your regular job because of the part-time pet sitting work? When you take responsibility for other people's pets, they need to take priority.

- Can you stand adding two extra hours, maybe more, to your work day? Unless your pet sitting service extends only to your neighborhood and you can walk across the yard in your slippers and pajamas to do your work, you will need to be ready for work and on the road earlier than usual. And you will need to stop and take time to tend to the pets under your care at the end of your long work day. If you are always just busting to get home, slip off your shoes, and relax with a glass of wine in front of the television, adding an hour to the end of your work day may not be the right thing for you.

However, research shows that pets have the ability to cheer us up, make us smile, get words out of people who haven't talked for years, and allow elderly folks to remain active as a caretaker. The positive benefits of interacting with animals is well documented, so maybe tossing a ball for a client's dog for a half hour after work is just what you need to get to your own home in a better mood!

> **Tip...**
>
> **Smart Tip**
>
> If you have an employee, you need an EIN—Employer Identification Number—issued by the IRS. You can apply online at www.irs.gov. Or you can send in form SS-4. It is simple, fairly quick, and absolutely necessary for anything but the simplest sole proprietorship.

Don't Zone Out

Don't ignore local zoning ordinances about what you can do when it comes to operating a business out of your home. And don't assume just because the guy up the street operates an accounting business from his home that it's legal to do so or that the same rules apply to a pet sitting business. The accountant may be operating legally, but your home may come under different zoning even if it's just a few yards or blocks away from the self-employed accountant.

Typically, if your business doesn't need to have a sign posted at the end of your driveway or doesn't require clients coming to your home, you are probably going to be OK. Your home business is operated in much the same way as the woman who is in field sales for a big company and works out of her car, rarely goes to the corporate office.

Best Practices for Small Businesses

When running a small business, there are several "best practices" that will help your business lean in the direction of success. Here are six:

1. *Give money the respect it deserves.* You do not have to be embarrassed about making money and you should not be shy about collecting it. Unless you are set up as a nonprofit (no easy task), no customer should expect a business to be unprofitable. Set your fees at a rate the market will bear and that will bring you the cash flow you need to create and maintain a good business. Give this little service away or that half hour of time consulting on the phone for free and you are eating away at what time you have for good paying customers.

2. *Create a business plan, no matter how small your business start-up will be.* A business plan gives you a guide to base all decisions on and against which to measure your success.

3. *Borrow as little as possible but as much as you need.* Undercapitalization is another reason small businesses fail. You need to be able to keep your business running in order to get customers to bring in revenue and make your business a financial success. The two most substantial expenses in your pet sitting business will probably be for a suitable vehicle and to create marketing materials. While the latter can be made lless expensive these days with simple desktop publishing programs and a basic printer, doing them takes time. A car is definitely a top priority.

4. *Maintain health insurance.* If your spouse has a job that provides benefits to you, awesome. But don't be without at least catastrophic insurance that would cover large hospital and emergency bills. If at all possible— although it's not easy for small-business owners—also maintain a disability policy that provides some level of coverage if you are injured and cannot perform the type of work that you do. This is typically quite expensive and isn't necessary if your coverage is not needed by your family. But if it is, do some research and find a policy. (See Chapter 6 for more information on this.)

5. *Be realistic about how much business you take on.* Burn out is one of the top factors in why small businesses close down—the owner/manager simply wears out! This often happens within the first 18 months. While this is not to say that any small-business owner can afford to be accused of being lazy, committing 18 hours a day, six or seven days a week is exhausting, plain and simple. If your plan is to start up your business,

make it phenomenally successful, and sell it within two years, perhaps this will work. But if you are planning to be in it for the long haul, building up gradually and perhaps selling in 10 to 15 years, start slowly with a few customers and increase your business as you gain experience.

6. *Hire employees sparingly.* Employee's paychecks as well as contributions for social security, worker's compensation, and unemployment taxes add up fast. When you think you need an employee, do a thorough financial breakdown, preferably with your accountant, and make sure the employee will pay for himself through either increased or more efficient business in a relatively short time, say within six months. Do thorough interviews and get references from any potential employee so it doesn't become a nightmare.

Complying with the zoning ordinance for your town or part of town may be as simple as filing for a permit at a modest fee. Go to the town hall and ask the questions. Don't ask questions only of the town clerk. Ask the chair of the zoning board, perhaps talk with the planning board chair, and someone on the zoning board of adjustments. It can't hurt to cover all your bases. It is not worth spending money setting up your business only to find out that you can't operate from your home.

Phoney Stuff

Beware!

While growth is the desired goal in any business, be sure your business growth is not too fast—too many customers, too many expenses, too many employees. All businesses measure growth in a different way, sometimes differently at different times. Measure your growth regularly and always use your business plan as a guide for growth.

You will, of course, need a phone line. Don't use your home phone—you will not instill much confidence in a potential client if your nine-year-old son answers the phone and responds with the classic preteen "uh, huh" and "I doan know." Tell your family they should not answer your business phone. If your "office" is in the middle of the family area, you may want to turn the ringer off while you are hanging out watching television in the evening.

Buy a phone with an answering machine that can hold a professional greeting. And then create a professional greeting! You can use "voice mail" provided by your phone service, but do not use the kind that offers only a prerecorded greeting by a stranger that makes no

▲

personal reference to you or your business. I can guarantee you that this kind of message will cause a significant percentage of customers to wonder if they got the right location and hang up and try the next pet sitter listed in the phone book.

Get a business line. A business line costs more than a simple residential line, but it will give you a listing in the business section of the phone book, which usually pretty quickly pays for itself.

And, although this will be repeated in the marketing chapter, while we are on the subject of phones, do be sure to have at least a listing in the "yellow pages" of the phone book.

Do You Need a Business Plan?

The answer to this question is plain and simple: yes. A business plan can help ensure a well-organized business with few, if any, surprises. It can help you get start-up or expansion capital by showing the viability of your idea or the ways your business has met its expectations as mapped out in your business plan of three years ago.

A major function of your business plan will be as a road map for you to keep on track with your planned destination, both at the macro and the micro level. If you

---

Business Plan Information

Information about writing a business plan abounds. Many of the books listed in the Appendix contain sample business plans. Don't expect to simply use an existing pet sitter business plan and plug in your name in all the appropriate places. Find one whose format appeals to you and mimic the format in your own business plan.

Much of the general business-related stuff is the same in all business plans, such as the state of the economy and how to fill your customers needs, but from there you fill in the details as they relate specifically to pet sitting. In fact, be sure your business plan reminds readers at all times what kind of business you are starting. Also be sure your business plan is a suitable length for the size of the business you plan to start. A part-time business in which you intend to service a dozen customers does not need a 60-page business plan. That would make as much sense as a 23-year-old recent college grad heading out job hunting with a five-page resume.

---

refer to it often, it will help you see immediately where you got off track and allow you to get back on track before you get too far astray.

There are many sources for getting help with business plans (see the Appendix). Here are the basic elements you need in your plan:

Summary

This is where you succinctly spell out just what business you are providing. This is not where you go into details or spend time trying to convince the reader that your business is a good idea. Simply offer an overview of what your business is.

Industry Overview

Provide information here on the pet sitting and pet industries. Statistics on number of dogs/cats per household, how often pet owners tend to solicit pet care service, and how the spending on pet care has increased dramatically over the past decade is convincing information that your business idea is a viable one.

Your Credentials

Include not only your animal-related credentials here, but also your experience in small business and business in general. You should include your resume somewhere in your business plan, which you can refer to here. But you should elaborate on some of the jobs you've had and the skills you've acquired that will help you in either running a small business or caring for pets. Those skills can be marketing successes, especially measurable ones, or new projects you helped launch that went on to be a success, or even examples of projects that required exceptional time management.

Operating Overview

This section will cover exactly how you plan to set up your business, such as whether you will have an office in your home, whether you plan to rent a storage space, and if you plan to have any help.

Financials

All good business plans have financial projections of at least three and preferably five years out. Your forecasting can certainly be modest, but you will want to show annual

Bright Idea

If you are thinking of hiring someone to help out, check your local community colleges for a veterinary technician program. These are good places to post notices and you will increase your chances of finding a dedicated and knowledgeable pet person!

▲

Your Trunk Office

As a pet sitter, you will be working out of your car much of the time. Buy a portable file holder and keep copies of all your forms in your car. That way you'll have them on hand when you see your clients. Keep a "desktop" in the car—a stapler, tape dispenser, pack of pens, paper clips, and Post-it® notes at the ready. Bring only those files for the clients for whom you are working that day, however; that kind of personal information is best to keep close tabs on.

improvement or at the very least hold your own over the first three years. Your financials will include spreadsheets on revenue projections, expense projections, and a balance sheet showing the difference between the two.

Start-Up Costs

Start-up costs on a pet sitting business should be modest. The one major outlay you may have to consider is reliable transportation. If you are driving a 15-year-old truck that it takes a screwdriver to start and ten gallons of gas just to make a trip to the nearest grocery store, you are going to eat up your profits fast if you ever get to your pet sitting jobs to begin with! Pull in the yard with that vehicle and you are not going to impart a warm feeling of confidence in your potential client. Consider purchasing a practical sedan with a hatchback that gets 35 miles per gallon. Lease returns are very popular for used cars these days—they are only three years old and have reasonable mileage because the lease puts a limit on the number of miles the leasee can put on the vehicle.

A car like this will not only make clients feel confident that you will be able to show up at their place while they are gone, but it is not so new that they are concerned you won't take Fido to the park daily as agreed because you don't want a dog in your car.

Forms

You've now learned that as a pet sitter you need to be trustworthy, reliable, well groomed, and possess incredible time management skills. Don't stop trying to reach perfection yet—in order to be successful in this business, you also need to be organized.

One way to keep youself organized is to use a few common forms. The start-up expenses worksheet on page 26 is a good example.

Client and Pet Profiles

These are the forms that hold information about the clients and their pets. The _____ ion, such as name, address, and home and work

_____ or separate sheet or file card for each pet—the _____ iled because the pet is who you will actually be _____ name, his feeding schedule, amount and type _____ like water in the dry food or not, etc.

_____ at tells if the pet takes any regular medication _____ t he takes at what intervals, how it is typically _____ s bought, especially if it is a prescription drug), _____ and if he is currently sick or suffering from _____ r your care. You want to know how old the pet _____ e lay around the house all day or is he usually _____ strangers? You might also make a few notes of _____ for the initial consultation.

_____ et any specifics about the household—is there _____ using it? What day is garbage pickup? What _____ f you agree to do any basic home care things _____ e mail, make notes on those things, too.

_____ency Care

_____ nd clear—it shouldn't be so complicated and _____ ind the key emergency information you need

_____ form on half a normal-sized sheet of paper. _____ he number for the animal control officer in _____ t owner for where they will be *for that visit*. _____ t. Chances are that the pet owner will leave _____ rator or the counter, but you also want it in _____ d it.

_____ groomer on the card—skunk spraying is one thing that comes to mind that could constitute a grooming emergency!

You will surely come up with a few of your own as you go along, but there are a few that are important. Be careful not to create so many forms that you need a form to keep track of the forms.

Start-Up Expenses Worksheet

Pre Start-Up	Cost
Market research (phone calls, subscriptions to trade journals, trips to veterinarians, professional association memberships)	$200
Legal and accounting services	500
Start-up advertising	100
Web site design	500
Equipment	
First aid kit	$80
Dog leash and collar	20
Dog muzzle	20
Cat litter box/litter	15
Mace	10
Office Furnishings and Equipment	
Computer/printer (optional)	$1,200
Desk/chair	200
Cell phone service (first six months)	300
Forms/business cards/invoices/paper, etc.	200
Subtotal	**$3,345**
Miscellaneous (roughly 10%)	$350
Total Start-Up Expenses	**$3,695**

Basic
Services

Any service business needs to offer certain basic, expected services. Pet sitters also need to have a core offering that your customers expect. The three most basic services that you will provide for pet owners are

1. feeding.

2. making sure the pet gets out to do his business.

3. getting the pet some exercise.

In this chapter we'll concentrate on dogs and cats. Despite the things you read about pot-bellied pigs, pet tigers, and other highly exotic animals, the most common job you will get will be caring for a couple of the more than 100 million dogs and cats that currently call our homes their homes. Eva and Dorothy of New York, say that although they care for all kinds of pets, their most frequent requests are for dogs and cats. Even if there are other animals like birds, fish, or hamsters in the mix, Fido and Fluffy will almost definitely be the basis for your pet sitting visits as well. (That said, you'll find some specific information on other common house pets in Chapter 9, livestock and barn animals in Chapter 10, and more "exotic" pets in Chapter 11.)

The Real Goal

Pet sitting is appealing to owners because it means their pets will be able to stay in their home environment. Although the pet's owner is not around, the pet is likely to feel more secure in familiar surroundings than in a kennel where things are confusing and unfamiliar. (For some pets this is more important than for others, but most pets do appreciate being in their home territory.)

With that as the main criterion for hiring a pet sitter in the first place, it is important that you are able to maintain as close to a normal routine for the pets under your care as possible.

You may want to segment your fees into half-hour time slots, but often a half hour is too short and an hour is too long for a home visit for the basic one dog or one cat pet sitting scenario. Forty-five minutes seems to be a good amount of time to spend time with the pet and then do some cleanup (litter box, shaking dog blankets, etc.) while the pets eat. Then one last "walk" before you go. And of course a pat on the head and a smooch!

You also need to consider the time it takes to get to the job and back. This is discussed later in the chapter, but you will want to come up with a distance range that is included in your fee and then any mileage beyond that is a surcharge. And at some point, the customer is simply out of your market range and you can't take on that customer at all.

> **Tip...**
>
> **Smart Tip**
> Have the owners write down the brand and type of food their pets eat. If it's an unusual brand of food that is not found at most grocery or convenience stores, be sure they also leave info about where they buy the food.

Feeding

One of the most important services a pet sitter provides is making sure the pet is fed. Again, being able to feed according to the pet's normal schedule is ideal.

Expect the owner to provide the food. In case they don't leave enough, be sure to have the owner write down what brand and type of food the animal eats (see Chapter 2 on setting up some forms for basic information gathering). No animal should be abruptly changed to a different food at any time least of all when he is under the stress of his owner being away.

Having the owner write down the type of food may seem unnecessary—if you empty the bag, of course you can just read the bag to see what kind of food the pet eats. However, many owners transfer their pet's food from a bag that you tear open on the top to a resealable container to retain freshness and keep pests out. You may come to the bottom of the container and find that the bag is nowhere to be found! Also, if the food is somewhat unusual and not readily found at the grocery store, be sure to have the owner write down where they purchase the food. When it comes to pet sitting, you want to do your best to avoid surprises.

In Chapter 2 you learned about making up a file for each of your clients and each of their pets. Write feeding information in your file, but be sure to check with each job to see if the pet still eats the same amount and type of food. Dogs have been known to develop allergic reactions to foods over time and veterinarians sometimes recommend starting the dog on a new type of food, which may have happened since your last job with this client. Also, pets go on and off diets almost as often as people do so the quantity of food may have changed since you last sat for the pet.

Details, Details

Also be sure the owner tells you where things are like can openers, plastic can lids for unused portions of canned food, scissors for opening bags, anything they use on a daily basis to feed their pet.

Make sure to ask about idiosyncracies. "Does Fido like water in his dry food?" "Does Fluffy like her canned food mixed in with her dry food, or does she like them served separately?"

Questions like these can mean the difference between Fluffy eating or going on a hunger strike while her owner is gone. A simple thing like where the animal normally eats can be an issue. Many herding dogs—like Border Collies and Shelties—are very sensitive to noise and vibration. If you put my Border Collie's food dish next to the refrigerator instead of by the back door, she may not go near it at all simply because it is in a different place, depending on how hungry she is. But she definitely won't eat if the refrigerator is running! One of the main points of hiring a pet sitter as opposed to depositing the pet at a kennel is to simulate the pet's common routine, so you need to know that routine.

Multiple Priorities

The placement of food dishes and which dish goes where on the floor first can be especially significant when you are sitting more than one pet. Two dogs will have a definite pack hierarchy. If they eat the exact same food, that can be less important—whichever bowl of food hits the ground first is the one the top dog will be eating.

However, if you are feeding two dogs two different foods or you are feeding a dog and cat, bowl placement can be critical. Some dogs will never touch the family cat's food, although I have never owned one of those polite creatures. Cats rarely consume all their food in one sitting so you may find that you are feeding the cat on top of the washing machine in the laundry room (which also wouldn't stop our Labrador Retriever . . .).

Be sure the owner gives you a rundown of the routine, and if you aren't provided with a detailed list, take some notes yourself.

Water, Water Everywhere

Do not forget water, an extremely important part of the feeding routine. There is not a pet on the planet that doesn't need 24 hour access to water. You cannot leave enough water, put down two bowls for the dog or cat in case she spills one or something unpalatable drops in one. Attach two tubes of water to the hamster cage just in case one loses its vacuum and all the water leaks out. And change them every feeding.

Be sure to find out from the owner approximately how much water the pet normally drinks in the course of a day. This way you will not only be sure to leave enough water for the pet, but you will also get a sense of whether the pet is consuming normal amounts of water or not which may indicate a health issue that needs attention.

Cats need water, too. Although most housecats that share the home with a dog will also drink out of the same water bowl, leave a water bowl specifically for the cat in the cat's eating area.

Doing Business

Another key job for the pet sitter is to be sure the pet gets a chance to do his business on a regular basis. This is more of an issue for dogs than cats. Cats will probably just use a litter box. But the litter box needs to be changed regularly in order for the cat to be happy about using it. It doesn't hurt to make two litter boxes available to ensure they stay relatively clean. However, many cats are very particular about the kind of litter box they use, so if the owner doesn't have two, you may not want to purchase every different kind yourself just to have the right one to leave as a backup.

Because of the litter box issue and because cats can be left large amounts of food, which they eat only when hungry (unlike dogs who tend to eat all that is put in front of them), cats often can be visited just once a day to fill up the food dish, change the litter box, and check in on the animal. The downside of this is that when cats are the sole house pet, owners often don't use pet sitters for their care. For short periods, cats don't need any attention and for longer periods like a few days, cats can be easily tended by the friendly neighbor. You might gain some cat-only clients by suggesting in your marketing and advertising materials that even though cats can be self-sufficient, it is important for someone to check on the cat to make sure it is OK and not sick or injured or stuck in the laundry chute.

Dogs, on the other hand, need at least two outings a day, preferably more. Although I don't know of a dog who has been trained to use a litter box, I'm sure it has happened. But don't expect it to have happened with one of your clients' dogs; it probably hasn't.

Be sure the owner lets you know the dog's usual schedule. Most dogs will urinate almost every time they go outside, so that is easy. But, as with the old saying "a watched pot never boils," dogs seem to not defecate if you are anxious for them to hurry up! So if you know the dog's schedule, you will better be able to time your visits accordingly.

Some dogs are in an environment where you can feed and put them out in the morning and then feed and put them in when you do your evening visit—and they will have had all day to take care of their business. It really depends on what the client's home and set up is and what they are comfortable with.

In the wake of highly publicized pet kidnappings and theft of purebred animals, many pet owners are not willing to leave their dogs out all day unattended. If it is a close neighborhood with a neighbor who is home all day, the pet owner may be more comfortable with that. But again, that may be the owner who will just hire the neighbor to take care of the pet instead of hiring you. In other words, be prepared as a pet sitter to get the more difficult jobs, not the easy ones!

Exercise

Most dogs need some daily exercise. Small dogs can get exercise just chasing a ball down the hallway. But even those easily entertained pups need to see the sunshine and get some fresh air every day. So dog owners will probably want their dogs exercised at least once a day. Some dogs can be easily exercised by throwing a ball or Frisbee® in the backyard, but others may need a vigorous half-hour walk to chill them out for the evening.

Try to do all off the leash exercise within a fenced area. If a fenced area is not easily available, get the owner's take on how best to exercise the dog. An extra long dog leash or even a long (30-foot) line used to exercise horses can be used to throw a ball or a Frisbee to a dog who remains attached to you without the danger of running away.

Get the Low-Down

There are some things you will want to know from your client before taking Rover out for a walk.

- Does he tend to get along with other dogs?
- What route do you normally take him for a walk on?
- Is there a house along that route that has a loose dog that I should be aware of?
- If it is winter, or windy, or rainy, does Rover normally wear a coat? Where is it?
- Do you typically use a choke collar or a harness or some other special equipment to walk Rover?
- Is there a fenced-in place where Rover could spend a few minutes off the leash safely?
- Do you bring along treats to reward Rover for obedience on the walk? (This may be especially important if Rover is a puppy.)

Cat Exercise

"Cat" and " exercise" aren't words that are put together very often. Cats seem to need very little in the way of directed exercise. In fact, they seem to prefer to move as little as possible after they grow out of their playful kitten ways. What exercise they do get to keep healthy they seem to be quite capable of providing for themselves—such as following the sun around the house by walking from the upstairs bed to the downstairs sofa. Running and hiding in the closet when the pet sitter comes seems to be another common cat exercise.

 Beware!

Don't attempt to walk a cat on a leash unless the owner informs you that the cat has been trained to a leash. Leash walking does not seem to be as instinctive to cats as to dogs and you could have quite a tangled mess on your hands. And if the cat gets really scared, you could have a much more dangerous situation with a cat who was frightened, bolted, got loose, and is now running around or at the top of a tree with a harness and leash attached to him.

Cats do like to play, even well into adulthood. They don't seem to do this as much for exercise as for entertainment. Taking a few minutes to dangle a stuffed mouse on a string or roll a ball with a bell in it can bring a cat a day's worth of joy.

Some cat owners take their cats for walks on leashes attached to harnesses. Cats usually need to be trained to walk on leashes—their first instinct seems to be to roll over and attack the thing on their backs!

Laundry Time

Depending on the length of time the owner is away, you may need to clean or change bedding—wash dog beds or cat beds or put fresh shavings in the hamster cage. Find out if it is OK to use the family washing machine for cleaning bedding (but never leave it running when you leave). The best thing is if there is a change of bedding so you can put clean bedding on dog/cat beds and take the dirty ones with you to do at the Laundromat (for a fee of course!). This may include not just the specific dog and cat beds, but also blankets and towels left on human beds and chairs.

Besides cats and dogs, other animals need cage cleanings and perhaps some "out" time. Birds may need to stretch their wings a little, rabbits may be accustomed to the run of the kitchen for fifteen minutes every day. Some rabbits have an outdoor cage for some daily fresh air and sunshine. Since the very concept of using a pet sitter is to give the pet the closest to its usual day as possible, you will be expected to fill in for all the things that the owner typically does with or for the pet.

Grooming

Significant grooming will be covered under "added services." Your basic service should include everything the owner does on a daily or several-times-weekly basis. For example, your basic service does not need to include nail clipping for dogs—this task is commonly done once every three or four weeks, so unless the owner is gone for a month, this should not have to be your task (although you most definitely want to add it as a service for an extra fee). However, if the dog or cat is long haired and the owner tends to give the pet a quick brushing daily or every couple of days, you will definitely be doing that as part of your service. This is where charging by the hour or charging by the visit of a set time length can be wise. You will get an idea of how long it takes to do the basic pet sitting service—feed, walk, change litter box—and that is your "basic" visit. Anything that takes you more than that half hour or hour warrants an extra fee. Anything that makes use of your specific expertise and credentials should be accounted for as a separate expense.

In other words, anyone can run a brush through a dog's hair for three minutes. But if you are expected to groom the dog, doing special trimming of hair or nails or tooth brushing, these are extra and need to be charged separately.

In a later chapter we will discuss added services, but you need to determine what your basic services will be in order to come up with a basic fee. Add-ons are obviously over and above the basic services and can be provided in a kind of a la carte menu format, especially depending on the type of pet.

The Environment

Some of your basic services will need to take into account the pet owner's home environment. Does the large three-year-old German Shepherd need to be driven to the park three miles away in order to get a good romp? Can the 12-year-old Shetland Sheepdog run around the owner's fenced yard for 15 minutes and be ready for a good night's sleep? Does the owner live in a condo and walk her Samoyed three times a day and expect you to do the same? Your basic service may not include three visits a day, but if it does, your fees should reflect that.

Bright Idea
Give your clients a menu of services that you are willing to perform over and above the basic ones relating to the pet. Then let them "pick three" that are most useful to them and include these in your basic charge. Any others on the list that they choose can be charged at an add-on rate.

Mail Sitting, Newspaper Sitting, and Other Fundamentals

The pet owner needs to be away, perhaps over a long weekend skiing in the Rockies, or off on vacation for ten days, or away for the week on a business trip. She sees your brochure at her veterinary clinic when she stops in to buy pet food. She considers hiring you to come to her house twice a day while she is gone to tend to her two small dogs and feed her parakeet, but she can't commit to using your service. She's never used a pet sitter before, she usually takes Puff and Duff to the kennel. But the last time they were there, they got fleas. And it is a pain trying to fit in the time to run them to the kennel and pick them up between all that needs to be done to prepare for her business trip.

Your brochure says that, you also bring in the mail, the newspaper, and otherwise help make the home look occupied. That's the clincher. She can not only leave Puff and Duff in their home environment, but she can also take comfort in knowing that someone is stopping by her vacant home twice a day.

These little extras can bring you customers. Don't promise the moon—don't promise to bake cookies for the neighborhood fundraiser that she will be out of town for or shovel the whole driveway or stay for the afternoon while the plumber works on the bathroom because the only appointment she could get was while she was away. If you want to have a viable pet sitting business, you can't be a property manager for all of your customers! But you can offer those little perks that are more applicable to your pet sitting service.

For instance, when you are walking Puff and Duff, go down the driveway and pick up the mail and newspaper on the way in. You'll definitely want to do things like check the thermostat in the winter. If when you feed the dogs, no water comes out of the spigot, you'll either call the homeowner or the plumber, depending on how you arranged emergency things with the owner. While you don't want to be property manager, you also don't want to ignore these things. A malfunctioning furnace can simply be dangerous to the pets, so it is related to your job. If no water is coming out of the faucets, a simple call can mean the difference between a repair and disaster. Your clients will reward you with a bonus or, preferably, more business if you go that extra mile.

How Much Is that Doggie in the Window?

Figuring out how much to charge for your services can be difficult. It seems like it should be as simple as figuring out how much time you will spend, and figuring in some gas money.

That is the basic premise. You do need to get an hourly rate, and you need to pay for your expenses. But some expenses are hidden. You need to be sure you are charging enough to cover those hidden costs as well.

One thing to be aware of is that you can't predict how many jobs you will have throughout the year. You may have 50 clients on your mailing list, people for whom you have actually done pet sitting. But of those 50 clients, perhaps only 30 will use your services in the course of one year.

Unfortunately, some expenses are fixed no matter how many clients you have. Insurance, licenses, association memberships, subscriptions, ongoing education, and a vehicle all cost you money each year whether you have one client or 100. Your fees need to accommodate those expenses while not pricing yourself so high that you dissuade customers from hiring you.

How Many Clients Are Enough?

It is key that you figure out how many clients you can reasonably handle. Break your clients down into basic categories. There are at least three:

Day Care

Perhaps the least consuming visits will be day care clients. Dog owners, for example, who work long hours and hire you to come by perhaps late in the afternoon, let their dogs out, and give them their evening meals. Even long-term cat sitting can require only one quick visit a day to feed, change the litter box, fill the water bowl, and make sure you get at least a glimpse of Fluffy to see that she seems well.

Long Weekenders

Other clients may be people who go away on long weekend vacations a half dozen times a year. They are the ones who would rather have Fido stay in his home where he is more comfortable. They may feel that bringing Fido to a kennel and picking him up when they get back is just too much hassle for a weekend away. By hiring you to come to their house, they can leave on their trip right from work on Friday and come back whenever they want without having to time their return around when the kennel is open to pick Fido up.

Business Travelers or Extended Vacations

Some of your clients will be businesspeople who are away on extended four- and five-day trips during the week. They may be called away on a business trip without a lot of notice. Or you may have clients who go on a couple of seven- to ten-day vacations once or twice a year. These you should get plenty of notice for, but both the business traveler and the extended vacation traveler will require similar amounts of time and similar revenues and expenses.

How Many of Each?

Unless you really plan to focus your business on one type of client, you will want to have a mix of the above three. A mix will provide you with a reasonable cash flow and a reasonable variety. And they all won't need your services all at once, so if you can keep a good mix, you can keep yourself in work much of the time.

The day care clients will consume the least amount of time overall, but by nature they need attention every day. The long weekenders will need a significant amount of time over that long weekend, but they are customers only five or six times a year.

Business travelers can be the most time consuming. Businesspeople have traditionally chosen not to have pets because of the unpredictability of their day. However, with the increase availability of pet sitters, even businesspeople with very hectic schedules can have pets in their lives. And they often have the discretionary income to hire pet sitters on a regular basis.

Not only will business clients require a bit of your time, but they will probably also need you to occasionally be available on a moment's notice. That means that while they can be lucrative customers who need your services often and are not only willing to pay decently but also are willing to pay a surcharge for last-minute service, you still can't take on too many of them. You simply won't have the time.

So What Do You Charge?

Many factors go into deciding on your fees. The main consideration—location— is going to mean that fees can be wildly different around the country.

But logic dictates that if you are a pet sitter in northern New Hampshire, your fee schedule is probably going to be a bit lower than in southern California. And if you are in a rural area anywhere, your fees will probably need to be lower than in metropolitan areas where people are closer to higher-paying jobs and have come to expect things to cost more than in the country.

Your Salary Expectations

One way to look at pricing is to figure out how much you need or want to make for income. Here's an instance where your business plan becomes a very important tool—go back to it and see what kind of revenue projections you indicated for a specific time period.

Say your business plan showed that with the third year of Pet Care Is Us you plan to make $25,000. If you start with that figure, you can break your revenue down from there. If you have accumulated 75 clients in three years, each of those clients would have to be providing you with, on average, $325 per year in business in order for you to meet your goal. But maybe in year two you decided that you wanted to take on a line of pet care supplies to sell. In its second year, your third year of business, that line, your business plan says, should bring in $8,000. That means your pet sitting services, to meet your projection, now need to provide only $17,000 of that $25,000 projected revenue. Now your 75 clients need to cover a smaller amount of that overall income, averaging only $226 per client. Of course, that's only if you plan to bring in the same amount of revenue three years running, which you do not.

But using our type-of-client breakdown above, you can start to break that out even more specifically into how much of that $17,000 will be brought in by each type of client and, therefore, come up with a new average per client within those categories. So if Ms. Business Traveler represents $8,000 of that $17,000 total, and you have 20 business traveler clients, your average per client for that category will be $400.

Break down the other two categories similarly. After you get those totals, you can start to figure out how much time per client is spent on each type of client, and then how much per hour you are making from that particular type of client.

The Numbers Can Tell a Lot

Once you break your information down in this way, you may start to see that you need to get more of a type of client or less of another. Or you may realize you should charge more for some clients who are taking even more of a chunk of your time than you realized.

Putting Your
Best Paw Forward

Pet sitting, like many service businesses, relies on having a large stable of customers in order to be successful. Even if on average each customer hires you once a month for two days, you need many customers to have a successful business. The good news is that the overhead is low—more customers do not mean much more overhead outlay, except perhaps gas to get to the customer's home.

Marketing Basics

The definition of "marketing" is basically to get word of your services to the group of people who may be likely to hire you. For pet sitting, that means getting word out to pet owners that you are available to take care of their pets.

How you do that is typically through two marketing vehicles:

1. Paid advertising
2. Distribution of print materials

Before we get into those specifics, let's talk a little about the concept of a customer base.

Building a Customer Base

In order to keep revenue flowing, you need a steady stream of customers. In the pet sitting business, this means figuring out how often people may be likely to hire you and then with that in mind, coming up with the size customer base you need in order to maintain the amount of money coming in to cover your expenses and create a profit.

License to Market

The list of licensed dog owners is public information that can be obtained from municipal offices. Try marketing to these lists because they represent a high percentage of your target market. Conscientious pet owners who might enlist the services of a pet sitter are the ones who would follow their town's rules for licensing their dogs, which also typically requires proof of an up-to-date rabies vaccination.

Create a flier. It can be as simple as an enlarged version of your business card. Fold it in thirds and add a catchy phrase to the outside of the flier to entice recipients to open it. Then mail it to licensed dog owners and the phone should ring!

The Chicken or the Egg?

Only you can decide whether you want to figure out how much money you want and then go get the customers that are required to cover it, or to get a customer base and figure out how much money you can make.

If you are doing this for the income, you will probably want to come up with an annual figure you would like to bring in. Then build your business to meet that income. The only way you can build that business is through customers.

Finding Customers

The most common way you will find customers is by word of mouth. If you are doing pet sitting part time, your place of employment and those of your family and friends will probably be good sources of start-up customers. If you are planning to start up your pet sitting business as a full-time venture, you will still want to tap your family, friends, and the places they work for potential customers. But to build a customer base and keep a steady stream of jobs will require broadcasting your services across a wider range than friends and friends of friends.

The Marketing Plan

A successful business starts not only with a business plan, but also with a marketing plan. Things you will want to consider are:

- a selection of printed materials and a list of places to distribute them.
- paid advertising.
- well-timed press releases.
- online marketing.
- other marketing vehicles such as speaking engagements or volunteer work.

Don't just create all these things and then leave them to collect dust on a shelf in your living room. Have a plan for them before you create them! Decide what use each marketing component will serve. And decide when to use them. Set up a marketing calendar and follow it.

> **Tip...**
>
> **Smart Tip**
>
> Amy C. of Amy's Animal Care in Maine has created an information packet that she sends out to potential customers who call inquiring about her pet care service. The packet includes her price list, information sheets on how to find a pet sitter, how to help your pet sitter give excellent care, and a bit of promotion on why you should hire her including a business card refrigerator magnet.

Printed Marketing Materials

Every business can benefit from marketing materials such as business cards and brochures. Here are the usual suspects and how you can use them specifically in the pet sitting biz.

Press Releases

A press release can be a simple avenue to free publicity. Send a press release announcing the opening of your business to every newspaper in your market range. Don't send the press release just to some general fax number. Send it to several editors—the business editor, the lifestyle editor, the Sunday edition editor, and the news desk. This should definitely garner you an interview and an article on your start-up business in at least one of the papers.

Press releases can be great publicity generators at other pertinent times, too. Here are some ideas:

- About a month before school vacations, send out a press release talking about the importance of remembering to line up care for Fido during the busy vacation season.

- Keep tabs on research and when a new report comes out send out an information sheet describing the health benefits of keeping Fido fit and trim, and discuss what you do to help keep dogs exercised.

- Send out information tips about pre-flea season or how to keep your pets safe during the hectic holidays. This kind of thing establishes you as a pet expert and gets your business name out there.

Business Cards

Many computers come loaded with Microsoft Office. Within that program is Microsoft Publisher. This desktop publishing software has a business card template and uses a "wizard" to walk you through creating your own business card. Purchase a pack of Avery or some other brand of business card stock, prepunched usually in six-up format, and print them out on your home printer using even just an inkjet style printer. You can create a professional-looking business card in literally minutes; there is no reason not to have a supply of business cards on hand at all times.

Many other business card software packages exist as well, most of which include copyright-free clip art that allows you to jazz up your business card with pet-related graphics and photos. You can even scan a photo of you and your pet or pets and drop it into place on your business card—a very personal touch with a great message about your knowledge and love of animals.

Even if you want to have the local copy shop or one of the office supply stores create your business card for you, it is not a huge expense. And they will have a larger array of logos, graphics, and fonts for you to choose from than your basic desktop software.

Be sure to design your card to reflect the kind of business you have. If your pet sitting service does not include large animals, do not use a horse for a logo. This is simply misleading and confusing. On the other hand, you don't have to have a photo or graphic of every kind of pet you are willing to care for. Your business card can hold a fair number of words that explains your service. For instance, Tanya K., a pet sitter in New Hampshire, has almost 60 words on her business card! Not only is it still highly readable, but the card covers a great amount of information about her service and her credentials. Tanya's card includes her business name, phone number, and e-mail address and reads:

Time of Pets

Dependable, Friendly Care
at Your Home or Barn
While You Are Working or Vacationing

Pet sitting services include daily visit(s) with playtime
Exercise, feeding, trips to groomer or veterinarian
Barn care including stalls, feeding, grooming, turn-out, and more!
Fully insured
Red Cross Certified in Pet First Aid
Call for a Free Consultation
222-333-4444 or e-mail TimeforPets@abc.com

That's a huge amount of information, and she includes four pictures to boot! It's all on a coated card with a blue background, an easy to read typeface, tons of information, lots of style and the extra cute factor. This one stands out in a crowd.

Business cards are small by nature. A dog or cat graphic can provide the most immediate representation of your business, but if you are willing to provide pet sitting for almost any type of animal, find a line that gets that across. "Any type of house pet welcome" or some other simple line gets across that you don't do barn animals but you would sit for an iguana.

Unless you have a physical office, you won't need to put your address on the card. But do be sure to include all contact information including your business, fax, and cell phone numbers as well as your business e-mail address. If you have a Web site, by all means be sure to include it.

Having business cards in your wallet or in a special holder is one thing, but you need to get in the habit of handing out a business card to everyone you meet. With more than half of all American households having pets, it is a good bet that whomever you give a business card to may be a prospective client.

Business cards are also handy for posting on bulletin boards because they take up little space and will be more likely to be left up for the long term. And they make easy and inexpensive ads because many publications offer a "business card section" for advertising.

Slogans

We'd like to interrupt this discussion on print materials for a brief word on slogans. A marketing slogan is a good thing to come up with. You could spend a lot of money and hire someone who has marketing experience to come up with your slogan, but that seems best left for Coca-Cola and other multibillion dollar international companies. For a small business, there is probably no one who can come up with a more perfect slogan than you.

That's not to say you can't solicit ideas from friends and relatives. In fact, have a pizza party with the specific intention of bantering slogan ideas around for your new business.

You'll notice that Tanya K., pet sitter from New Hampshire, uses a simple slogan on her business card seen earlier in this chapter: "Dependable, friendly care." That's about the most important stuff that a pet sitter's potential clients may want to know.

When you come up with it, use it everywhere—on your business card, brochures, phone message, even at the top of your invoices.

Brochures

Tri-fold brochures can also be easily designed and printed on your home computer. This is where you can provide lots of information to prospective clients about you and your services. Have these brochures ready for any local chamber of commerce event you attend, for bringing to trade shows, dog shows, or any other venue where pet owners gather. Some veterinarians will let you leave a stack in their waiting area, depending on how much room they have. Use them in displays like those the local banks often offer where local businesses who have accounts with the bank can have a display table for a week in the bank lobby.

Brochures are great tools for spelling out the details of your business, from your specific services to a price list. Create yours as a self-mailer so when someone calls and asks for information, your voice message reminds them to leave their address so you can add them to your mailing list. Then you can print out a label and mail it to them immediately.

Mailing brochures can provide that three-hit marketing tool that can make the difference between a new client or not. Hit one: The prospective customer calls and either gets you or your nice voice message. Hit two: They receive your brochure in the mail within a few days of calling. Hit three: You follow up with a call and/or they can look on your Web site, which is listed prominently on your brochure and business card.

Some of the things you want to cover in a brochure:

- *an overview of your business.* Just a couple of paragraphs will do. Tell when the business was started and why.
- *your biography.* Be sure to include why you chose this business. Feel free to talk about your own pets. In fact, make sure you do. Include a picture of you with your pets if you are computer savvy enough to make that happen. Also talk about your business abilities and other background that builds that trust and confidence prospective clients need to feel about you before they hire you.
- *a list of services.* What do you offer? In-home visits, feeding, exercising, grooming, litter box changing.

Fliers

A flier can be simply your tri-fold brochure that you post on bulletin boards. Or you can make a single sheet small poster-type flier that you tack onto bulletin boards. They do take up a little more space, but if you make your flier attractive, it can be a great marketing tool when posted in appropriate places. Fliers like this are especially good for posting an upcoming event that you are holding or sponsoring, or some special notice like a one-year anniversary special.

Include those convenient little tear-off strips on the bottom of the page so people can take your number with them. Make the strips wide enough that you can include a line like "pet sitting service" or your company name, if it is self-evident what you provide, above your number. People stuff those little strips deep into their pockets—and they pull them out several days later when they are cleaning out their jeans pockets before sticking the pants in the wash. Chances are they won't remember what the number was for—but if you add your little tag line, they will do an "Oh yeah, this is that pet sitting service that sounded perfect for when we go to Montreal that long weekend in September." They just might give you a call!

Be sure to freshen up your fliers on a regular basis. There is nothing that says "probably no longer in business" than a flier that's dated, faded, ripped, curled, and rained on. If the flier looks old, potential customers will probably think you haven't been around to change them because you are no longer doing pet sitting.

A Web Site

It is imperative for businesses to have a presence on the Web. Your Web site will provide all sorts of information and added value to your business. Potential customers prefer to check out your Web site to see all the details about your business before picking up the phone. Your Web site can spur them on to call and line you up for their next out-of-town trip.

The Web site should, of course, include any and all information about what your pet sitting service provides, why your services are so great, and how to get in touch with you, and other useful information that will pull them in:

- Contact information such as name, phone number, and e-mail address
- A bio about you and about any independent contractors that you use (don't include their direct contact information, you don't want to potentially lose business directly to your I.C.s)
- The history of your business
- A menu of your services and a price list
- A list of the animals you are willing to sit for
- Information, such as pet care services you provide
- Links to any veterinary clinics, groomers, pet supply stores, feed stores, and other businesses that refer clients to you

While the site should certainly be fun and attractive, don't make it so complicated and take so long to call up individual pages that people don't want to spend much time there. Make sure your home page tells all the basic information: if they go no further than the home page, they will be able judge your style, know your basic qualifications, and know how to reach you. Don't let a Web page designer go overboard with your site. Pet sitting is an uncomplicated service business for the most part; you want to make it appear that way.

Beware!
Paid advertising can be a money sucker. Good ad salespeople can readily make you think that if you advertise in their newspaper or magazine, your sales will skyrocket. If you decide to spend money on paid ads, be sure to use a method that helps you track response. Coupons, "clip this ad and receive a free gift," or other specials related only to that ad are good ways to do that.

Paid Advertising

Advertising in this business depends on how many clients you are willing and able to take on. If you are well-connected in your local pet industry, you will probably get all the clients you need from word-of-mouth and never need to spend a penny on paid advertising.

However, make sure to get a listing in the Yellow Pages. You don't have to spring for the display ad, but a line listing under your subject heading is going to bring in some business. Sometimes this basic listing is included in the cost of your business line.

You could ask the pet store, even if it's a chain, if you could produce a blow-in card and pay per piece to have the card blown into their fliers for a certain distribution area. These fliers are usually pretty well sortable by zip code.

Other places you can advertise are pet-related newsletters. The local animal shelter typically publishes a newsletter that it sends to all of its contributing members. Ads are typically very cheap for a year-long contract.

Newspaper ads may be prohibitively expensive; it depends on the circulation of the paper in your area. Most newspapers recognize the value of providing an opportunity for small businesses to advertise in their papers and create specific small-business ad pages. These often consist of business card-sized ads that are very reasonable in price, especially if you can spring for ongoing placement.

Another advertising vehicle that is within the price range of a small business is the classified magazines. These usually offer commercial listings at higher rates than the personal listings that the magazines mostly consist of but are still reasonable. Some of them also have display ads. Just be sure their range stays within the service range of your business.

Vehicle Sign

This is a tricky one. The value of having a magnetic sign on the door of your vehicle is great—to do pet sitting, you do a lot of driving around and lots of people will see your ad.

However, the downside is that it may not be in the best interest of your clients to have your vehicle with your business sign on it sitting in their driveways. Pet sitting is a signal to anyone passing by that the house is temporarily vacant. People go to great pains—cancelling the paper for the length of their vacation, postponing mail delivery, having interior lights and even radios on timers—to make their home seem occupied and they probably wouldn't appreciate your blaring message—"Hey, these people aren't home, so I am taking care of their pet a couple of times a day!" in the driveway for a half hour to an hour.

One other consideration is insurance. The difference between having a personal automobile insurance policy and being required to purchase a commercial policy may be as simple as whether there is signage on the vehicle. (See Chapter 6 on insurance for more information.)

Association Memberships/Web Site Links and Searches

Membership in local associations—the chamber of commerce, a pet sitters' organization, a veterinary-related group—will not only provide you with some great ideas and moral support, but also customers. Bring a stack of business cards to chamber of commerce meetings and don't leave until you've handed out most of them. Remember, pets are part of more than half of all American households, so don't assume someone is not a potential customer or a potential referral just because their business isn't pet related. If they don't have pets themselves, their relatives, friends, acquaintances, and their employees do!

Be judicious in your membership in national associations. While dues are typically modest, be sure the association is worth all the extra mail, and probably e-mail, that you will receive. It won't take long for you to realize that the schedule of a pet sitter doesn't allow for much active participation in associations. But many of them offer services like your name on a list on their Web site where people from all over the country can search for pet sitters by region.

Likewise with getting your Web site linked on other Web sites. Think broadly when it comes to Web sites of businesses within your market area. Again, the business itself may not be pet related but many of the workers at the business own pets. You would be best to limit this kind of marketing to those businesses that hire professionals who would be making a high enough salary to afford pet sitting services. Think of businesses that have employees such as salespeople and lecturers who would be on the road a lot and potentially in need of someone to care for their pets regularly.

Web site linking is often set up as an exchange. They put a link to your site on their site, you link their site on yours. And if that at first doesn't make sense, remember that pet owners need health insurance, car repairs, and rug cleaning as well as things directly related to pets!

Newsletters

Newsletters can be a wonderful marketing tool but the key to a successful newsletter is to keep it simple—and useful. Provide your clients with important information regularly, including

- *When you are scheduling vacations.* This gives your clients a heads up about when you definitely will not be available. An important thing here is that they will use this information, if at all possible, to not plan their own trips during times when they already know you won't be available—and you won't potentially lose a good customer to some other pet sitting service.

- *Ideas that can help you in your care of their pets.* For example, a form they can cut out that lists all important phone numbers that they can post near their phone.

- *Pet care tips.* Pet owners who are dedicated enough to hire pet sitters for their pets are also dedicated to providing quality care for their pets. They will read just about anything to glean more information on how to take care of the animals they share their home with. Provide something of use in every newsletter—health-care tips, feeding information, grooming ideas, some current research, etc.

- *Coupons from local merchants.* Merchants love simple ways to advertise their businesses, especially if you will do it all for them. Offer to put a business card-sized ad in your newsletter in exchange for being able to offer your customers a discount or a coupon to use at their business. Everyone wins this way—your customers get something of value, they think kindly of your business because you have offered them something of value, and the business owners gain new customers by getting people in their store.

Speak!

Giving seminars on pet care or speaking at local pet club gatherings can be time consuming, but it is a very focused way of marketing yourself and your services. You will be speaking directly to groups of people who are

Tip...

Smart Tip

If you like to write, are good with deadlines, and can fit in the time, approach the local weekly about writing a pet-related weekly column for their paper. This is a great way to get your business name in front of your target market. And the column gives you automatic credibility that will give potential customers one more reason to call you before they call the next pet sitter listed in the phone book.

your target market: pet owners. And pet people hang with other pet people, so the net you cast is much wider than the group of people sitting in front of you.

Being a speaker and offering seminars also gives you additional credentials that you can add to your list of impressive credits—that you are knowledgeable enough about pets and pet care to speak about your expertise to others. Be sure to get a press release out about any speaking engagements you are lined up for—it is a great opportunity to get your business mentioned in the newspaper.

Offer to speak to a group at the local animal shelter—perhaps with the marketing pitch that if people are hesitant to adopt that pet they've always wanted because they are worried about how to care for the pet when they have to go away, you can offer some tips. Have a handout available to which you can staple your business card so they not only have your name and number on the handout, but they can pass your business card along to a friend or colleague.

Start small on the speaking thing and build up to larger audiences if it interests you. But be sparing in your speaking engagements—you'll want to stick to your target market area if it is to be beneficial to you, and you don't want to wear out your audience!

Try Something Different

People with pets are found in all sorts of places. Not only do they buy pet food at the pet store and bring their pet to the veterinarian, but they also go to the dentist, the library, and the grocery store. Just as with thinking about Web site link exchanges, think out of the box when it comes to where you post your pet sitting signs.

The rule of thumb is that people need to see and hear things three times for them to really register and remember. Say a pet owner sees your posting at the grocery store on Saturday, then again at the local convenience store Wednesday evening when she stops for the paper on her way home from work. Then three weeks later, she decides to go away for a long weekend and she asks the veterinarian for a name of a trustworthy pet sitter and your name comes up, the potential client will think "oh, yeah, I've seen a posting for Any Pet, Any Time pet sitters a couple of places now. They seem to be very businesslike, getting their name out there. And my vet recommends them, so I'll give them a call." And just like that, you have a new client.

Useful
Credentials

Small-business owners often have to be the proverbial "jack of all trades." Fix the computer printer, make coffee, do the bookkeeping, and do the actual business of the business! In any small business, the business owner has an equation to balance.

One side of the equation is your knowledge of your specific business—in this case, animals. Do you know how to feed animals? Are you knowledgeable enough about their health to know when something is wrong? Do you know how to interact with the types of animals that will be under your care?

The other side of the equation is your business knowledge. Do you know how to write a business plan and keep it updated to help guide your progress? Do you know how to record your expenses and your revenues? Do you know how to be businesslike with your clients?

In order for pet owners to want to hire you to take care of their pets, the main thing they will want to know is that you are dependable. You will need references and referral sources that attest to your reliability, trustworthiness, and responsibility. These people will need to be professionals and "publicly known" people such as veterinarians, community leaders, etc., not personal family and friends who would probably be completely unknown to the potential client. (That said, if you and your prospective customer have a friend in common who would give you a good reference, that is a legitimate name to give.) You will also want to buff up your resume with some certifications and licensings, which we will talk about later in this chapter. But probably more important than any piece of paper is that your potential clients will want to know you have experience with pets.

Firsthand Experience

The best way to have experience with pets is to have pets of your own. Flaunt it if you do. Instead of some little cartoon animal on your business card, include a nice photo of you and your happy-looking pets. There is really no better credential for a pet sitter than being a pet owner whose pets seem content and well cared for.

Having pets of your own means you know how important it is to the pets' owners that they are taken care of properly. When we take on pets, we take on the responsibility of taking care of their needs because they cannot do this for themselves. When we bring them into our houses, they cannot go foraging for food and find water, we have to be sure to provide it for them. They cannot let themselves out to relieve themselves, we need to make sure they are let out on a regular schedule. And pet owners relinquish that responsibility to you, the pet sitter, when they leave their pets in your care.

If you don't have pets, don't flaunt that fact. You must have great affection for animals to be successful in the pet sitting business. Chances are if you are considering this line of work, you do like animals, so prepare yourself with a satisfying answer when your potential client asks you if you have pets. Is your apartment too small? Does your landlord not allow pets? Perhaps you are grieving a pet you recently lost and aren't ready for another. Are you getting into the pet sitting business specifically because you love animals but can't have pets of your own at the moment so you are vicariously having pets through your clients? Whatever you do, don't tell a prospective customer that you don't have pets because they are too much of a pain to care for. That will turn off any self-respecting pet owner.

Licensing

No licenses are required to become a pet sitter. However, there are some written credentials that will enhance your appeal to potential clients.

Training

Have you taken obedience training classes, perhaps just to educate your own pets? Dog training classes can be not only a great credential for a pet sitter but also a potential add-on service (see Chapter 12 for more on expanding your business). Dog owners will be happy that you know enough to not allow Fido to jump all over you when you come to care for him—something they may have been trying to teach the dog for months, so if you let him jump you will greatly set back their training.

Also, perhaps they have been trying to teach Fido not to jump and they will pay you extra to work on this problem with Fido when you come to care for him. This way your visit can bring you a greater fee. This kind of training may well pay for itself in just a couple of jobs.

Best in Show

Another feather in your cap could be if you enter your own dogs or cats in competition. It doesn't have to be simply show competitions where your pet mostly competes at looking like a classic example of the breed. Agility work—where dogs go through tunnels and over fences and balance on teeter-totter-like boards at their owner's direction and under time pressure—has become huge in the United States. And working-dog competitions involving Border Collies or other stock dogs who were bred to work with livestock are getting almost as popular in the United States as they are in the United Kingdom and Australia.

If you do this kind of thing with your dog, you will get two benefits. Your clients will know you are a serious pet owner because competing with any animal takes commitment to the animal's health and training. Also, at competition you will be among many other dog owners who may be able to shuffle some clients your way!

Of course, it would be difficult to do any serious level of competition while establishing a pet sitting business—a lot of the competitions take place on the weekends, which of course is exactly when you will be most wanted for your pet sitting jobs. But if you are still in the business planning stages, you might consider adding something like competition to your resume, or if you have done it in the past, make sure to promote that! Successful competing is a better credential than if you and your pet never placed, but even if you didn't, the experience of competing brings with it a certain level of pet knowledge.

Grooming

Do you love grooming dogs and cats? Even if you don't want to offer this service to your clients, knowing that you do it or have some training in it will also let pet owners know that you have experience. That experience isn't restricted just to grooming itself—in order to groom a pet you need to know how to handle the animal. That kind of hands-on experience can be very valuable to pet owners.

You may not want to go into full-fledged grooming services, but you can offer some of the simple things like a basic brushing, nail trimming, and simple clipping of ears and feet.

First Aid Training

The American Red Cross offers a training program for pet first aid. While it is directed toward the pet owner, it is a perfect training program for a pet sitter to take and offers additional peace of mind to pet owners who hire you.

The program teaches students how to react in a number of emergencies, including choking, CPR, bone fractures, and other emergencies such as being hit by a car and natural disasters. It covers basic health parameters for dogs and cats, some bird information, and even some on other small mammals and reptiles, all of which you may find under your care.

Check with your local Red Cross chapter for a pet first aid training program near you. The Red Cross also offers a first aid pet book and an instructional video done by the Greater Los Angeles Chapter. The American Red Cross Web site is also helpful at www.redcross.org.

If you take the Red Cross Pet First Aid Training, be sure to add it to any visible marketing you do for your pet sitting service.

Check Chapter 12 (on expanding your business) for further details on serious grooming services and what you need to get started. A real boon to a service like grooming is that it will lead you to pet sitting clients and vice versa.

Be a Techie

With the explosion of pet ownership has come an explosion in the need for veterinary services. And for every veterinary clinic, there are several technicians needed. To fill this need, veterinary technician programs are springing up all over the country. And as of this writing, their student numbers are growing in leaps and bounds.

Pet owners are spending more than ever before on their pets, from basic veterinary care to high-quality food to surgery and other serious conditions including medication. Technicians play no small part in the overall pet care picture.

Amy C., a pet sitter from Maine, is a licensed veterinary technician. She spent time as a practicing LVT in a veterinary clinic. This not only added considerably to her credentials, but also the requests she got to pet sit from customers when she worked at the clinic made her think to go into the business in the first place, and the clinic itself became a great source of client referrals. "Being a vet tech means a lot to people," Amy has found.

Licensed technicians go through a two-year training process in which they learn how to give shots, do first aid, recognize diseases, etc. In fact, although the amount of education required is less than in human nursing, "vet techs" are the RNs of the pet world; licensed technicians can do everything but offer diagnoses, perform surgery, prescribe medications, and give prognoses. Techs do a lot—take X-rays, administer medication, draw blood, and much more.

For those interested in specializing, there are programs beyond the two-year degree. However, for the purposes of running your own pet sitting business, you probably don't need to get this far in depth (or in debt!). The specialties tend to be in things like radiography, anesthesia, orthopedics, and other more medical-related areas that you will not find much of a call for in the pet sitting world.

With the veterinary technician credential comes great trust from clients. You can take on more complex situations, like pets who have had surgery and need day-to-day care in the home during their recovery—a licensed vet tech doing home care can offer a great amount of relief for the working pet owner. You can charge more for these services than for routine care. And you can feel a great sense of satisfaction from your work, which involves a lot more than simply making sure Fido does his business.

Even if you don't find much need (thankfully) for heavy-duty medical services, just knowing how to clip toenails or administer medication or simply having a general idea that something is wrong will boost your credibility as a pet sitter.

Visit Your Veterinarian

If you don't have the time, money, or inclination to go the licensed veterinary technician route, spend some time with your veterinarian. Ask if you could pay a fee for a couple of appointment times and have him show you things like how to give the different kinds of shots (subcutaneous, or under the skin, and intramuscular). Learn about good restraint practices for dogs and cats, emergency procedures, and administering pills. Your veterinarian can also give you a list of common diseases or conditions to watch for.

Don't keep this to yourself. While "spent an hour with my veterinarian" isn't something you would put on a flier, do mention it to prospective customers. Not only does it show that you have learned specific techniques from a professional, but the fact that you made that effort at all shows that you are determined to give high-quality care to your customers.

Nutrition

There are no licensed credentials for pet nutrition. However, you can do many things to learn more about it.

- Tag along with a pet food salesperson and find out more about the different kinds of pet foods. Salespeople love to tell what they know—and telling it to you can help them refine their presentation to their customers.

- Read up on all sorts of nutritional information such as just what a dog or cat or bird needs for nutrition and specialized nutrition like vegetarian diets for pets, the use of raw meats, and the value of supplements. All the major pet food manufacturers (Science Diet, Iams, Purina, for a short list) have Web sites with good information about nutrition in general and their products specifically.

- Go to your local feed store and pick up literature on all the various pet feeds. (Bring your SUV—many feed stores carry dozens of pet brands each of which has dozens of varieties).

- Go to classes or seminars put on by local schools, pet-related stores, medical facilities, or shelters. If you live near a university that has an equine studies program or a large-animal hospital (that would be either a hospital for large animals or a large hospital for small animals), they often put on seminar series or workshops on animal nutrition. Also check with pet organizations.

Business Credentials

Your business probably won't warrant a Dun & Bradstreet listing, but even the smallest business can benefit from certain affiliations.

Chamber of Commerce

Become a member of your nearest chamber of commerce. If you are in a very small town, you will need to join the COC in the nearest "city." Of course, you want to be sure it is in your market range because one thing you will get out of the COC is potential customers; you don't want them to be so far away that you have to spend all your earnings in gas just to get there.

But besides the benefits you get from being a COC member, it is one more way to show to the world that you are a professional and you understand that being businesslike is important no matter what business you are in. So while a COC membership itself is certainly not going to sway a potential client one way or another whether to have you care for his cherished pet, remember that pet sitting is a business of trust—a COC membership is just one more thing on the list of trustworthiness. You are willing to get your name out there, and see and be seen.

Better Business Bureau (BBB) Standards

The BBB offers comprehensive standards by which they feel businesses should abide. Some of these that relate to a service business like pet sitting are

- ○ truthful, nondeceptive advertising.
- ○ price comparisons of identical products/services from competitors.
- ○ use of "free" for giveaways that are unconditional.
- ○ disclosure of any extra charges.
- ○ ad designs that are clear to the customer and minimize the possibility of a customer misunderstanding the offer or message.
- ○ use of objective, not subjective, superlatives: for example, "the best" tends to be a subjective superlative since everyone's opinion of what is the best can be different. An objective superlative may be "the only pet sitter who offers obedience training." The BBB expects you to be able to back up any such claims.
- ○ use of endorsements and testimonials should be actual and not fabricated, and should be used in the context in which the testimonial was given.
- ○ any claims of performance or quality of care should be backed up by data.

Better Business Bureau (BBB)

The Better Business Bureau is a watchdog organization with the consumer in mind. The BBB requires that you be in business at least six months to join and your business must meet their rigorous standards (see sidebar). The BBB is where customers register complaints and the bureau will investigate those complaints and report on their findings. Anyone interested in doing business with you (or anyone at all, for that matter) can look at any complaint received by the Better Business Bureau about your business and the BBBs findings.

Again, not a deciding factor in itself, but one more notch in your favor if your potential customers see that you are a member of the Better Business Bureau. Pet owners simply will not take chances with their pets.

Pet Sitters International

Pet Sitters International (PSI) is a professional association for pet sitters. Their comprehensive Web site includes some great information and links to other useful sites. They offer information on medical benefits, using employees and subcontractors, and other things you will want to know. The site (at www.petsit.com) is very helpful for those just in the thinking stages.

PSI offers education and accreditation programs. For around $300 you can take their Pet Sitting Technician program, or the advanced program, and a couple of other levels and gain accreditation from this international organization. They provide certificates for you to display, pins to wear, and other items that signify your education as a pet sitter.

In order to be accredited by the organization, you need to supply them with the appropriate information, including

- your business license (if required in your state).
- marketing materials, including a brochure and business card.
- a service contract and other forms such as an emergency plan.

PSI also offers liability insurance and bonding for members. To contact them, check their Web site or write to Pet Sitters International, 201 East King Street, King, NC 27021 (336) 983-9222.

Rounding Out Your Resume

You certainly want to flaunt any professional experience you have had in pet-related jobs. If you have worked for a veterinarian, don't just hide that fact on page two of your resume—include it in your marketing materials! You don't have to include the name of the veterinary practice, but you should say that you have worked at a veterinarian's office. Working with a veterinary practice is great not only for gaining some expertise, but also for getting referrals for your pet sitting services. Pet owners are quick to ask their veterinarian for that kind of information.

Insurance and
Legal Matters

Since pet sitting is just about caring for cuddly animals, there is no need to worry about insurances and other legal protections, right? Wrong! You always need to be sure you protect your own assets such as your savings, your house, and your car. It just makes sense.

A pet sitting business involves all the legal issues that are pertinent to any small business as well as some issues that are unique to pet care.

Insurance

There are several types of insurance you will want to consider and a few you will want to make sure to have. Some, like health, are personal insurances, but others are more business oriented like liability insurance, bonding, and workers' compensation.

Liability Insurance

You will definitely need to be sure you are fully insured with liability insurance that will cover you in the event that, say, a pet dies while under your care and the owner decides you are responsible for the pet's death and sues you. But there are other potential instances of liability that you may not think of until they happen.

Beware!

Don't assume that just because you have insurance you don't need to worry about things that can lead to lawsuits. You should be reviewing your policies and revising your contracts and other legal agreements at least annually to be sure that they still reflect your business as it now stands. Set policies about how you handle people's pets. Keep your automobile safe and maintained, and never transport a client's pet unless it is confined in a crate or safety harness. Insurance companies will expect you to take appropriate measures to avoid lawsuits to begin with.

Smart Tip

Tip...

Amy C. of Maine recommends that all pet sitters, especially those who take clients' dogs for walks, learn how to break up a dog fight. There are very specific techniques described in Chapter 8. Liability surrounding injury to other animals and the pet you are sitting is considered in the contract in Chapter 8.

For instance, what would happen if the client's dog bit a child while you had the animal out exercising him in the park? The dog may have been to the park every day for the past five years and played happily with all the children, but it only takes one day, one child, and one bite for a potentially nasty lawsuit.

A rider on your homeowner's policy is typically how small businesses with extremely low revenue and a modest amount of foot traffic to the home cover their liability insurance needs. However, for a pet sitting business where most of your business is done offsite, you need a separate liability policy.

Bonding

Nicknamed "honesty" insurance, bonding is this mysterious little insurance policy that you need to get for any business where you are entrusted with valuables, like the key to someone's home and all the contents in it. Bonding ensures the client that you are trustworthy, and if they prove otherwise, the insurer provides them compensation.

Disability

Any self-employed person should attempt to obtain disability insurance that covers you if you can no longer do the job you are trained for. For instance, if an injury makes you unable to drive for an extended period of time, you will want disability insurance that at least covers you for some amount of time until you can either retrain yourself for a different occupation, redirect your business, sell your business, or resume your business at the level you did before you were injured. Disability insurance can be very costly and difficult to get. If you do get it, don't ever give it up!

> ⚠ **Beware!**
> Don't take on pets with what is in the legal world called "known propensities." In other words, if the dog has been in the court system because the dog bites, you will be putting your business (and yourself, and perhaps your employees or others) at risk of being bitten. Of course, we all know that most dogs bite because of very specific circumstances. But in the courts, it doesn't really matter why the dog bit if it has had a reputation for biting before—you can easily risk your insurance company not covering you because you took an undue risk.

Health Insurance

Many self-employed people scrimp when it comes to health insurance. Yes, it can be a big chunk of money each month to pay the premium. But it takes just one major illness to put you under financially.

First, depending on the illness, you won't be able to work at all or maybe not at the level you normally do. This instantly means a reduction in your income.

But secondly, a huge factor is the medical bills. With good insurance, you can mostly take this factor away except perhaps in the case of something catastrophic like paralysis.

If you really calculate it, paying, say, a $300-a-month premium for insurance that has a low ($10) co-pay and will cover other things like chiropractors, physical therapists, eye care, and other add-ons, will ultimately pay you back if you take care of yourself and use these medical professionals. Regular physicals, blood work, and a couple of visits a year to a chiropractor can all add up pretty fast.

Do consider dental insurance as well. It's actually not too expensive. In fact, at around $50 per month, two cleanings, check-ups, and annual X-rays will probably add up to the $600 per year that the premiums cost. And if you need more significant dental work, you will already be beyond the often two-year window that you must have had the insurance for before you can do certain major dental procedures.

Auto Insurance

Be sure to check your existing auto policy to see if it covers any accidents that might happen while you are using your car for business purposes. With some agencies, it will require that you get a rider on your policy. Some agencies won't cover you at all. A more likely scenario is that you will need to take out a commercial policy on your vehicle.

Liberty Mutual insurance company, for example, requires a commercial policy if the automobile is registered in the business name. If the auto is registered in your personal name, you would only need to insure it under a "business classification" only if the vehicle had business signage on it.

Also, be sure to check with your auto policy for any special circumstances for transporting other people's pets (Liberty Mutual, for instance, requires no additional riders on the basic auto policy). In other words, what would happen if you had an accident while a client's pet was in your car? Pets are usually legally considered to be "property" of their owners. If the pet were, heaven forbid, to die in the accident, the owner would be compensated for the pet's monetary value, which is typically only the amount the animal is actually worth as a pedigreed (or not) animal.

Of course, we hope none of these things will ever happen, but by being protected you don't have to learn the consequences after the fact.

Smart Tip

Tip...

Find an insurance broker who will look for the best insurances policies for you. Some brokers deal in only one or two types of insurance, but they have access to information at their fingertips that would take you hours and hours of research to dig out. The insurance broker will also come to know your priorities—for instance, whether you want the best health insurance for a reasonable cost or whether you simply want it as cheaply as you can get it. At renewal time, your broker will send you a menu of options and recommendations based on her knowledge of the current status of the insurance market and what you need or want out of a policy.

Legal Issues

Covering yourself legally is important in any business. Don't let the pet part of your pet sitting business sway you into thinking that you are just feeding the cute little poodle, what legal issues could possibly come up? Let me assure you, there are lots.

You will be taking the risk on yourself if you were to get bitten by a client's pet. This means you should be careful about the clients you take on. And you should take all precautions and learn as much as you can about handling whatever animals you agree to care for. Having certificates of completion from a respected dog obedience school and the like won't stop you from getting sued, but they would help demonstrate to a jury that you take your responsibilities seriously, that you know how to handle dogs, and that this particular situation was a fluke and not the result of inadequate knowledge or negligence on your part.

Corporate Structure

The first major legal decision you made about your pet sitting business came way back when you were setting it up and you decided how your business would be structured. Your main choice was among the following

- sole proprietorship
- partnership
- incorporation

The choice you make will have a huge impact on how any legal issues are handled and resolved. The choice of sole proprietorship makes things the most simple—and it also means that all of your personal belongings are at risk. Incorporating is the most complex, but it is also more expensive and more complicated when it comes to legal issues.

Service Contracts

Many people who start a small caretaking business like pet sitting feel uncomfortable with having customers sign legal contracts for services. If you are one of these kinds of people, get over it. A written contract for your services makes it clear what services you will provide, when you will provide them, what is expected of your client, when payment is expected, and what happens when payment is not made in a timely manner.

The contract should include an outline of your fee structure, a limited liability statement, and how and when services will be rendered. You can also include a warranty.

Don't simply buy a pad of legal contracts at the local office supply store—your business is unique, and you will want your contract to reflect that. It is almost imperative that you hire an attorney to draft your contract. While attorney's fees can add up fast, they are well worth it for a customized service contract that you will use over and over. And as your business matures and expands, you can have your attorney tweak your contract to include any changes in your business.

In Chapter 8, you will find a service contract (see page 97) used by an existing pet sitting business as well as a couple of other forms that help clarify things between you and each of your customers. Look them over to help prompt your own thinking about what you need on your own contract.

Some potential legal issues should be addressed in your contract. The contract should make the following points:

- What should happen in the event the pet gets seriously ill and needs veterinary care? Who decides what to let the veterinarian do? What is the owner's attitude about extreme measures?

- What should happen in the event the pet dies?

- The owner should confirm by his or her signature that the pet has not been cited for having bitten someone in the past. Stay away from clients whose pets have bitten; it's unfortunate and most of the time the pet has been provoked, but it is ultimately a fact that pets who have bitten once are considered dangerous and likely to bite again.

Again, don't wait for these things to happen before you address them. In the emotional and sometimes heated aftermath of an event like a dog bite, you will wish you had thought things through ahead of time.

Employees

If you want to keep your business simple, avoid hiring employees. But if you want to grow your revenue and expand your services, employees will probably be a necessity. Employees do complicate a business from legal requirements to taxes to personality conflicts.

There are other ways to get help when your business is expanding beyond your ability to keep up. Subcontractors (who work for themselves, not you, also called independent contractors) can be a great interim (or permanent) step to taking on more clients. But in any service business, you will need to pick your subcontractors very, very carefully. They are, after all, representing you and the hard work you have done to create a certain level of care and a business flair and personality.

Noncompete and Confidentiality Agreements

If you hire a subcontractor, that person probably also contracts her services out to other pet sitters, either in your market area or outside it. You don't want your subcontractor telling her other employers any details she may learn about your business while she is filling in or taking overflow work for you. A confidentiality agreement would also cover things like not providing copies of contracts and other forms you have created (or paid someone else to create) for your business.

Noncompete agreements simply state that an employee cannot start his own pet sitting business and usurp your clients. If you do not have employees, this is a non-issue. Subcontractors do not work for you, so it is difficult to institute much in the way of legal agreements. That said, you certainly should include a line in your sub-contractor agreement that states that your client list is the property of your business. However, chances are that many subcontractors are trying out the pet sitting business on your clients to see if they want to start their own pet sitting businesses. An honest person you hire to subcontract will let you know that this is his ultimate goal.

Nothing can actually prevent an employee or a subcontractor from soliciting your clients to draw them to their own business. However, a signed agreement is a legal document in which they explicitly agreed not to do this, so if they do, you then have to decide whether or not it is worth pursuing legal action.

Workers' Compensation

If you have an employee, you must carry workers' compensation insurance, which covers employees if they get injured while performing their job responsibilities. The purpose is to avoid lawsuits resulting from on-the-job injuries. Workers' compensation is administered under both federal and state statutes.

IRS Obligations

As an employer, you are obligated to withhold a certain amount for income taxes, usually a percentage based on the information the employer provides on a W-4 form filled out at hiring. You also must withhold Social Security/Medicare taxes (that famous "FICA" line on the W-2. Not only do you withhold the employee's share, but you, the employer, also contribute an equal amount totaling at the time of this writing 15 percent of the worker's salary.

But wait, there's more. With employees, Uncle Sam also dips into your profits by requiring that you pay unemployment taxes. Check the IRS site for the current amount you need to withhold. Your accountant can also help you keep track of all these requirements.

Lastly, you may need to make these payments monthly, depending on how much the total is. The IRS likes to make sure you keep up, and don't get socked with a huge amount due all at once that you can't manage to come up with.

If you are going to have employees, be sure to keep up with these employment-related tax payments. You can really see how it pays to calculate just how much additional business an employee is going to bring in and if it is worth the additional expense (don't forget to calculate in the expense of the additional fees to your accountant and, potentially, your attorney).

Ultimately, if your business growth is pointing to the need for an employee, by all means start the hiring process. But don't take on the costs unless they are necessary. Review your business plan regularly and be sure that employees are part of the plan and are necessary for the level of expansion and growth you hope to obtain by a given point in time.

People often get into a service business such as pet sitting because they enjoy the actual act of providing a service. Amy C., of Amy's Animal Care in Maine, says that she finds it rewarding to help people with their pets. Not only does she do caretaking for them when they are away, but as a licensed veterinary technician, "I also like being able to steer them in the right direction when it comes to training, health, nutrition, and medical needs. I see a lot of people spending money they may not need to."

Finding an Attorney

Don't wait until you need an attorney to find one. If you own a business, you will need an attorney at some point for something. Here are some ways to find the best attorney for you.

○ Ask friends and family for referrals.

○ Call and chat with the attorney or the office receptionist. Get a sense of how they conduct business and what kind of reception you might get if you call.

○ Make sure you pick someone who has small-business experience and will be more likely to be sensitive to the legal needs of a small-business owner.

○ You probably won't find someone with experience specifically in pet sitting, but look for an attorney who has experience in service-industry businesses.

○ Find out up front what the attorney's rates are, what the standard fees are, how payment is expected, whether or not you can pay with credit cards, etc. Don't let the money part of it, which can be substantial, surprise you.

○ Last, but far from least, be sure the personality of the attorney is of the type with which you feel comfortable and confident. You don't want to avoid consulting your attorney just because you don't like to talk with him or her.

When you start to expand beyond your personal time capabilities to provide the service, you are then mostly doing it for income. Only you can decide what your goals and priorities are.

Independent Contractors

You will probably get most of your outside help by using independent contractors, or subcontractors. This situation may be able to carry you through all your needs without ever hiring actual employees. Although subcontractors will carry their own insurance, you also need to be sure to add them to your insurance policy as well.

Financial
Considerations

If financial matters are not your favorite topic, that viewpoint must change when you decide to start your own business. Finances probably won't ever reach as high on your favorites list as animals, but all business owners need to become intimately involved with the finances of their businesses. You can choose to have someone else take care of the

▲

nitty gritty details, but you still want to understand the basics of your business's financial setup and what it all means to the success of your business. Because without a financial core, a business is not a business; it is volunteer work.

If you don't care about your business finances, you won't be in business long. You need to have the resources to maintain your vehicle and to simply buy gas—or the good credit to put gas on a credit card—to get to your jobs in the first place.

There are some things to decide about the finances of your pet sitting business before you actually start up. You should have your books set up and be ready to record expenditures and revenue as soon as you begin putting out or taking in money for the business.

Class Act

Tanya K. of New Hampshire has an accounting degree and worked in the field for many years. And even she still has someone else do her books! But she admits that it is critical to have a handle on the business finances end of things. "You at least need to be able to track your expenses," she says, as well as to understand why it is important to do so.

One way to make the accounting and financial framework of your business less daunting is to take an accounting class. Check with your local Small Business Development Center (SBDC), which may either offer small-business accounting classes or keep a list of classes offered through local community colleges or continuing-education programs at a local university.

Be logical when you sign up for an accounting class—don't sign up for a class that will cover information beyond your current need or ability to understand. You don't need to know how to read the financial report of a 60-million-dollar international company to run your $20,000 local pet sitting operation.

Another way to start learning about small-business finance is to take a class on writing a business plan—financial projections will be part of that plan.

Cycles of the Financial Moon

First, you need to decide what your fiscal year will be.

Sole proprietors should choose the calendar year as your fiscal year. Business income for the sole proprietorship will be reported as Schedule C on your personal tax return, which is filed according to the calendar year. (Don't worry, more on the dreaded "T" word later.)

Corporations operate under a different tax structure, and can choose a fiscal year according to the logic of their business/industry. The pet sitting business has two main busy periods of the year:

1. *Vacation time.* Although people take vacations almost all times of year, the summer vacation time will be the busiest since the kids are out of school.

2. *The holidays.* Thanksgiving to New Year's will be another key busy time for pet sitting.

Whatever fiscal year you choose, these two busy periods will be encompassed within them.

Keeping the Books

Unless you are setting up a pet sitting empire right out of the box, you should be able to do your own day-to-day bookkeeping. If you have ever had even the smallest business or if you have ever worked for anyone else, you have heard it before but it bears repeating: Keep every receipt for any dime you spend on the business. You don't have to carry your ledger around with you, but gather those receipts in one place and record them in your ledger at least weekly.

Set aside time for bookkeeping. These records tell you a lot about your business. You may notice patterns, expenditures that seem excessive, or other things that you could change to make your business more efficient.

The Checkbook

Your checkbook will probably be the financial tool you use the most in the beginning. Since pet sitting businesses often don't take a lot of capital to set up (unless you actually set up a boarding kennel, which we will discuss in Chapter 12 on expanding your business) you have to be careful not to fall into the trap of starting your business and simply using your personal checking account to pay for things and deposit income.

Get a separate checking account and designate it for the business. Pay for everything with it, even if you use the account's cash card instead of actually writing a check. It doesn't have to be a "business" checking account, another personal account will do, just give the business an account all its own.

Not only is it good for keeping accurate track of things, but there are also some psychological aspects to having separate accounts and ledgers for taking yourself and your business seriously. Have your business name printed on your business checking account—it does lend an air of professionalism.

The Old-Fashioned Way

If you like a pen-and-paper approach to things, you can keep your books using an old-fashioned ledger notebook that you can still purchase in any office supply store or stationery store. Set it up for expenses and for income. At the end of each month or quarter or whenever you have designated, you can hand these ledgers over to your accountant who will review them, balance them out, let you know how much you still have for capital in your checking account, and perhaps even make suggestions of how to better keep your records. Your ledger, if well kept, can tell you a lot about the day-to-day status of your business.

Software

Many software programs exist for easy setup of bookkeeping for your small business. Two commonly used ones are QuickBooks and Microsoft Office. There are others as well with less well-known names such as Big E-Z Monthly Bookkeeping for Small Businesses.

The main thing you need to keep in mind is that while these programs do many calculations and other useful things at the touch of a few keys on the keyboard, they still require you to set them up in the first place and input the basic information, both initially and on an ongoing basis.

So if you are thinking that computerizing your books and doing it yourself is the easy way out, think again. No matter which method you decide on, you will need to put down the tug toy and spend time on the bookkeeping end of things. Set aside a large chunk of time to start and then set aside time on an ongoing basis, maybe an hour weekly and a morning monthly.

Be sure to keep these software products up to date by logging in to their Web sites periodically or signing up for their automatic updates or reminders so you can keep

COGS in the Pet Sitting Wheel

As a business owner, you will hear a lot about Cost of Goods Sold, fondly known as COGS. Even though COGS says "goods," services are also included under that category. COGS differentiates from overhead expenses, which are fixed—COGS will increase with increased revenue because every time you provide your service, it costs a certain amount in expenses.

them as up to date as possible. Although the bookkeeping products probably won't have as much in the way of updates, the tax products will have constant updates.

If you know yourself well enough to know that you are not going to set aside this time to feed your bookkeeping software, then hire an accountant. The upcoming meeting with your accountant will encourage you to pull the information together, and you have a person who will be nudging you to keep the appropriate records and provide her or him with the information needed to keep your finances accurate and up to date.

Accounting Methods

There are two basic accounting methods: accrual and cash accounting.

1. *Accrual.* This method of accounting is used in businesses where inventory is a factor. If you take on a line of products to sell, you may think about using accrual accounting. However, even if you do, you might want to set up the product line as a separate business from your pet sitting business and do the accrual accounting only for that business.

2. *Cash.* Cash accounting simply means that you record an invoice as revenue when you send it out and you record an expense when you receive the bill that your business is supposed to pay. It is a very simple means of accounting.

Making a Statement

Businesses use several statements to get an overview of their business and their financial status. These are:

- *Profit and loss statements (P&L).* This statement allows you to get a monthly picture of where your business stands that month, for the year to date, and compared to this time last year (either for the month or year-to-date).

- *Cash flow statement.* This handy little statement lets you know how much money is coming into your business compared to how much went out.

- *Balance sheet.* The balance sheet balances all your business's assets against all its liabilities. How much you own is compared to how much you owe. This crucial statement lets you know how your business is faring financially at any moment in time, giving you the ability to make some changes to shift the balance more in your favor. There are things you can do to shift the financial balance more in your favor. Here are a few ideas:

  - Increase the fee for your services
  - Get a more economical vehicle

▲

- Reduce the range of your market (if you are spending too much time/money to get to your jobs)
- Increase the range of your market (if you aren't getting enough jobs/customers)
- Stop billing customers and require payment at time of service
- Find new suppliers of things you need to keep on hand

You will, by the way, have created all these for your business plan, although because at that stage they are not based on actual numbers, they are known as "pro forma" statements, or "projections."

Accountants

The bookkeeping and tax software may be enough while you are still quite small with just a few clients. But as you grow, you should consider hiring an accountant to help you keep your records organized, adequate, and useful. While an accountant is an additional expense, it is a worthy investment. You don't have to use the accountant on a daily basis. Quarterly is probably enough to begin with. You can always increase your accountant's input to monthly when you have reached a certain level of revenue.

The important thing is that an accountant will keep you on track with your financial framework. Tax time will be easier. Growth will be easier. Getting additional capital to expand will be easier. You can be ready to jump on unexpected opportunities instead of having to recreate your financial history first because you didn't keep very complete records and weren't able to analyze or present your business from a financial perspective.

Set up an introductory meeting with at least a couple of accountants. You want to pick someone with whom you are compatible. You can weed out a couple of possibilities over the phone. One key question to ask your potential accountants is what kind of small-business experience they have in general, whether they have any experience with service-based businesses in general and pet sitting businesses in particular. Then meet your finalists in person. There may be a small fee for this meeting, but it is well worth it to go with confidence into what you hope will be a long-term relationship.

Taxes

You can't get around it—being a business owner complicates tax time. This is another instance where having an accountant comes in handy. You need, however, to be sure your accountant is a *tax* accountant, not solely a bookkeeper. There are so many rules and layers to tax laws that having a tax-savvy accountant will pay for itself in sheer savings on aspirin alone.

In their attempt to become more customer-friendly, the IRS has a fantastic Web site that falls into the category of "more than you ever need or want to know." But if it involves federal taxes, it is there. You can download publications and forms to read on screen or print out, which can save you on the evening of April 15th if you are scrambling to meet the deadline doing your personal taxes.

One IRS publication that all small-business entrepreneurs should probably download or get a copy of from the IRS is the *Tax Guide for Small Businesses (Publication 334)*. Don't worry about remembering it all—although there will be a nonnegotiable test on April 15th of every year.

Beware!

Do not fall into the trap of never paying yourself out of your business earnings. While it is important for a start-up business to dump a lot of its revenue back into the business, burn out is one of the top reasons that businesses fail. So if you work 80 hours a week, you should at least take enough money out of the business checkbook to treat yourself to a spa visit or whatever you find will recharge your batteries for the next 80-hour workweek!

Auto Expenses

Because traveling to your clients is a large chunk of your expenses for a pet sitting business, you will need to keep very detailed records of your automobile use. Keep a mileage log in your car and get in the habit of using it every single time you slide behind the wheel!

You can record actual expenses for your vehicle—oil changes, tires, gas, etc. However, if you use the same vehicle for both personal and business use, it may be more expedient to simply use the IRS mileage rate (which, for the 2002 tax year, was 36.5 cents per mile, but check this every year because it changes almost annually) because otherwise you need to carefully differentiate between uses, determine the percentage of use the car gets for business, and use that percentage when calculating taxable expenses for new tires, etc.

The key point here is that with this kind of business, automobile use is a significant expense and you should be sure to record every possible cent. This is not only important for tax purposes, but this is one of those places where hidden costs can eat away at your profits and you can't pinpoint exactly where the money is disappearing.

Client Invoices and Receipts

Even if you require payment on the spot, you always want to provide your client with an invoice for your services. This allows both of you to keep a record of your visits. Conscientious pet owners who are hiring pet sitters most likely keep a notebook full of info about their pets' care and health and they will stick these invoices in it, so your work will be useful on all sides.

You will want to establish some method of invoicing and giving receipts to clients. Depending on how fast your business plan shows your business increasing revenues and adding clients, you may want to think early on about having client software that keeps records of your clients. If you are looking to have only ten clients for the first year, you could perhaps just create one using an existing software package on your computer. You probably don't want to spend the considerable money it would cost to install a business software package (like Cornerstone, created for veterinary offices, that generates invoices and estimates, accumulates client history, and lets you choose ID numbers for various services), so keep it simple in this regard. If you know some computer-savvy teen or college student, he or she could probably get quite a kick—and some spending money—out of creating a program for you.

These client-based software packages usually include the capability of invoicing. You assign numbers to each of your services and as the program asks you what to invoice for this client, you select the appropriate numbers for the services you provided and they automatically are listed on the invoice with an explanation and a price.

The other advantage to setting up this kind of program is the accumulation of client history. When clients call to book reservations for your services for their pets, you can look on the patient computer file and easily access all services you provided in previous calls. This allows you to personalize the call—"Does Fido still take phenobarbitol twice a day?"—which gives a strong impression of reliability and a good feeling about how well you pay attention to that customer's pet.

You can also potentially add on services by saying things like "Last time we discussed having me walk Fido twice a day to help him be less anxious while you were gone. Would you like me to try that this time?" And you tack on an extra fee for an extra half hour of your time or a fee per walk or however you choose to set up your fee schedule.

The point is that your good recordkeeping not only helps you organize your business from a financial standpoint, but it also gives you opportunities to excel at customer service and client relationship building.

Payment Options

Do you want to allow your clients to use credit cards and debit cards? There is an added expense for this, but it can be very convenient for your client. The advantage to you is that with a credit card you get payment on the spot or, with a debit card, you find out on the spot that the client's account doesn't have enough money—the card simply won't go through. This saves having taken a check that comes back to you a week later.

Establish credit card services with your business bank. There is a percentage fee (around 2 to 4 percent) for each transaction.

Policies

Every business that deals with customers (which is every business, small or large) needs to establish policies and they need to be adhered to rigorously. If your policy is to require payment at the time of service, you need to stick to that policy for every customer, every time. Of course, you will always come up with the exception to the policy, but if every instance is an exception, then there no longer are exceptions because there are no rules!

Policies often are focused on payment- and money-related things but there are other things you may find you need to have policies about, too. How many times will you visit any one client in a day? How many pets will you care for in one household? Perhaps you have a policy that you will not take on a job caring for any dog who has ever bitten someone or had a complaint filed against it. The customers in this kind of business are all unique; you will come up with your own things to have policies about. But stick to your policies or don't make them in the first place!

Collections

Speaking of policies, have a collections policy and absolutely stick with it. Don't let invoices add up. If you find that you are embarrassed and shy about asking for over-due payment, you need to get over it. You provided your part of the bargain, your customers need to pull through with theirs.

To avoid collections problems, look for signs that clients are having trouble paying you and try to offset it. If a customer took too long to pay, don't take on a new job for that client without at least a partial deposit. Too long to pay too many times should mean complete upfront payment or simply not taking on the job at all.

Paying Yourself

Alas, this comes near the end because the majority of small business start-up owners go quite a few years never paying themselves. They dump all their profits back into the business. If you can afford to do this, that's great—you should probably plan to do this for at least the first year, depending on how complex a business you establish.

But there does come a point when you want to give yourself at least some pay. If you are independently wealthy, then pay yourself enough for some mad money. If your spouse has a fantastic job that provides for all the family needs, great—pay yourself enough to do some home renovations or buy new furniture or go on a couple of vacations a year.

Service businesses aren't like other businesses in which you build something that can be sold and that is where you can eventually make money. You certainly can sell your business—to someone wishing to start up a pet sitting business. It's much easier to buy an established group of customers. However, if there is no entrepreneur wishing to buy an existing service business when you are wishing to sell, there really isn't much opportunity to sell it to an existing pet sitting business—they can just as easily wait for you to close your business and then be sure to have ads and fliers in places that will get in front of your customers eyes. In other words, they won't have to spend the money on buying the business, they can gain your customers' business much more cheaply.

So pay yourself something—there is some reward to feeling like your business is providing a financial return, even if it is just dinner out twice a week!

If you need to get a paycheck out of the business, you will need to decide how much your paycheck needs to be and then figure out how many jobs you need to take in a given period to pay yourself that much—minus expenses and some padding for the business, of course.

Obtaining Financing

Although a start-up pet sitting business requires only modest start-up funds compared to many other businesses, if you do need to approach a lender for a loan, having financial projections or statements in order and presenting them professionally as part of your loan request can go a long way. Applying for a loan can be stressful enough in and of itself, so being ahead of the game with a full complement of financial statements from your business plan will save you some headaches.

Start-Up and Operating Capital

There are two kinds of money you will need for your business venture:

1. *"Start up" money.* This is the amount of money you will need to begin to operate your business. The good news about pet sitting, and many service businesses, is that the capital needed to get up and running is usually quite low—in fact, it can easily be less than $5,000. Enough to create some marketing materials, set up a separate phone line, buy a few first aid supplies, take a couple classes, and get your car completely serviced.

   However, don't forget that you also need money to maintain your own daily expenses. The time that you are spending with your pet sitting business is time that you will not be spending making money at another job, so you need to be able to have some spending money to keep you going until your business begins to generate and accumulate some money.

2. *Operating capital.* This is the money that is required to keep your business running until it begins to generate revenue to run itself—i.e., the goal is for the business to create its own operating capital. Your start up capital should be enough to take you through until your business begins to generate money. But then you will need to have operating capital to keep supplies stocked, gas in the car, and any other needs depending on what services you choose to offer.

Raining Cats
and Dogs

As a pet sitter, the majority of your business will almost definitely be caring for dogs and cats. Some pet sitters will focus on barn animals, which we will cover in Chapter 10.

Sitting for a dog and/or a cat will often entail caring for the family gerbil, guinea pig, parakeet, ferret or rabbit. You can find out more about sitting for those animals in Chapter 9,

Other Common House Pets. You get a little heads up in Chapter 11 about more exotic animals that may crop up here and there, keeping your pet sitting experiences even more interesting than you might have imagined.

Basic Dog Care

We'll start with dogs even though pet cats outnumber dogs because, except for extended periods, most people with only cats as pets do not enlist the services of a pet sitter. The cat can be easily fed by a responsible neighbor, and most cats aren't too concerned about how often they see people, so socializing isn't an issue as it is with dogs. And of course there's the litter box situation.

The upshot is that you may well find yourself caring for a cat, but it is usually the family dog that is the primary sitting need. Because you are coming for the dog, the pet owner will also have you tend to the cat. So let's start with the more needy pet, the dog.

The basics of caring for a dog will be the same for all sizes and breeds: feed him, give him fresh water, make sure he gets time out to do his business, and provide him with a bit of companionship and exercise.

Feeding

Always feed the dog—any pet for that matter—exactly what the owner tells you to. During your initial visit you will find out where the food is kept. Be sure the owner has outlined the

> ## Beware!
> Always be sure to keep a dog's food supply somewhere the dog cannot get at it. Even if the owner assures you that the dog never gets into the food bag, animals act differently when their owners are away. The dog may get more bored than he usually does or may be stressed out by the fact that her owner is away and may do things he "never" does. A dog who has overeaten is a very sick dog, will require a trip to the veterinarian, may require her stomach pumped, and can even die from her stomach being too full and twisting.
>
> Likewise, put bread, cookies, and other edibles high up or in the fridge or store them in the microwave out of temptation's way.

details like whether or not the dog typically gets water in his dry food or whether his canned food is mixed with the dry or whether they are served separately. This can save the animal some stress and can save you some stress as well; you may worry that he is sick if he turns up his nose at his supper simply because it is not prepared in the usual way.

Here are some other things to ask the owner about the dog's feeding time:

Vaccination Requirements

People have different philosophies about vaccinations, but as a pet sitter it is your prerogative to require them. Dogs should have an annual 5-in-1 vaccine that covers distemper, hepatitis, leptospirosis, parvovirus, and parainfluenza. Also check state regulations on rabies vaccinations and require that your clients comply.

Cats should also be vaccinated annually for three diseases: panleukopenia, rhinotracheitis, and calicivirus. Cats should also follow a rabies vaccination schedule of one to three years, although few states as yet regulate rabies vaccinations in cats.

- Is the dog normally a fussy eater? If she is, you will know not to be alarmed if she doesn't wolf down her entire dinner in a flash.

- Is there a specific place the dog likes to eat? If the dog's dinner is always served in the same place, be sure to set the bowl there, too. Pet sitting is intended to help the dog be more comfortable when his owner is away, so you need to provide these little consistencies.

- If you are caring for more than one dog and they eat different things, do they need to be locked away from each other during feeding? You don't want them eating each other's food and being sick, especially if one gets a prescription-type dog food and one doesn't.

One last thing: Even if the owner tells you that the dog doesn't at all mind being approached while he is eating, don't bother unless it's absolutely necessary. Dogs can be very possessive about their food, and it is just not worth the risk of being bitten.

Water

Water is vital. Do not scrimp on water because you're worried too much might cause Fido to pee in the house. Cleaning up a little pee on the floor is a lot better than having a dog in your care get sick from dehydration or constipation. Find out how much he regularly drinks during the course of a day so you will know what is normal water consumption for the dog and leave double that amount each time you visit.

Poison Control Center

The ASPCA runs a poison control center. The emergency number is (888) 426-4435. There is a $45 consultation fee for which you will need to provide a credit card. They also have a 900 pay-per-minute number, which is (900) 680-0000. The poison control center can provide information on dogs, cats, livestock, and other pets

Treats

Find out what kind of treats owners give their dogs, where they are, and how many they usually get per day. Give the dogs only those kinds of treats unless you ask otherwise. Some pet owners are happy to have their dogs receive any kind of special treats; others are very picky about what their pet eats. No matter your feelings about what a dog should get for food or treats, this is not your dog.

Toys

Leave only toys that are allowed by the owners. Some toys that are billed as indestructible last only five minutes in the mouth of a vigorous dog. And only give toys meant for dogs—this includes flying disks. The plastic disks found in the children's toy department can be very hard on dog's teeth and gums. Lighter-weight ones are made especially for dogs.

Exercise

Most dogs need at least a few minutes of exercise every day. Simply being outdoors is healthy for them, just as it is for us. Ask the owner what kind of exercise the dog is accustomed to each day; if you can't simulate it (like if the dog is accustomed to a two-hour walk in the woods every morning), at least do something to get the dog some level of exercise. Little dogs can often get sufficient exercise simply from chasing a ball down the hallway for ten minutes, but they still can benefit from fresh air and sunshine.

Dog Restraint

Before we get into some basic first aid, you will want to know how to restrain a dog to perform simple procedures such as taking his temperature or transporting an injured animal. Collars, harnesses, and muzzles are all useful forms of restraint when dealing with dogs.

Keep in mind that dogs that are injured may react violently even to their owners, even if they are normally very friendly. They may be in pain or disoriented. Be sure to muzzle a dog that is injured—keep a couple of different-sized muzzles in your vehicle.

You can fashion a makeshift muzzle out of anything that has some length to it and is soft—a necktie or a rag, for example. Fold the item in half to make a loop and quickly get it around the dog's nose. Cross it under the chin and tie the ends behind the ears. Be sure it is snug enough not to come loose but not so snug at the throat as to injure the dog or cut off her air.

Vital Signs

You will want to know something about dog and cat first aid. The most basic is to know the animal's vital statistics and how to test for them. It's always nice if the owner has the animal's baseline vitals written down somewhere, but many owners don't know this about their animals.

Temperature

The normal temperature range for a dog is between 100 and 102.5 degrees, a little higher than humans. A dog's temperature is taken in the rectum. Although veterinarians are still stuck on the old mercury thermometers, digital thermometers that you can buy in the drugstore are easy to use and easy to read.

Dog Fight Savvy

Amy C. of Maine says that the most important thing you need to know if you take dogs for walks is how to break up a dog fight. "Very few people know the proper, safe techniques to do this," she says. If there are two people, each should grab one dog's hind legs. "The dog," says Amy, "may transfer its aggression to you so move the dog in a circle to keep the front end occupied." Amy recommends always carrying pepper spray. "This may seem harsh," she says, "but it is mild compared to what can happen in a serious dog fight."

▲

You will, of course, want to know that the dog is OK about this. Even if animals are normally even tempered, they may be a bit more testy if sick, so proceed with caution. Lubricate the end of the thermometer with petroleum jelly or another lubricant, or use little sanitary sleeves (a few are often provided with the thermometer), lift the dog's tail, and insert the thermometer about an inch. The digital thermometer will beep when it has remained at the same temperature for a certain period of time, indicating the highest reading has been attained.

Pulse

The normal pulse rate depends on the size of the dog. Larger dogs have a slower pulse. Check the pulse by pressing in the groin area inside the hind leg up near the abdomen. This is the femoral artery. Once you have located the pulse, count for 15 seconds then multiply times 4 to get the beats per minute. The normal bpm range for a large dog is 60–90 bpm, for a medium dog 70–110 bpm, and for a small dog 90–120 bpm.

Respiration

Normal respiration for a dog is 16 to 30 breaths per minute. You can test this by putting your hand to the dog's nose and counting the exhalations.

Capillary Refill Time

Another way to tell whether a dog is ill is to check how long it takes for blood to return to tissue. The best place to check this is the gums. Gently lift the dog's upper

---

Post Vital Signs

The following are average vitals for dogs and cats. Remember, all of these can be influenced by external factors such as excitement level and ambient temperature.

	Pulse (beats/minute)	Temperature (degrees F)	Respiration (breaths/minute)
Large dogs (100+ lbs.)	60–90	102°	15–30
Medium dogs (50–100 lbs.)	70–110	102°	15–30
Small dogs (less than 50 lbs.)	90–120	102°	15–30+
Cats	150–200	101.5°	20–30

No Chocolate! No Onions!

Pets should not be fed chocolate in any form. Chocolate contains a naturally occurring compound called theobromine, which causes a spike in adrenaline leading to a racing heart and even coma, depending on the amount consumed.

Another no-no for pets is onions, which contain a substance that can lead to anemia.

lip and press your finger to the gum to drain the spot of blood. Watch how long it takes for the blood to refill the area. It should refill immediately and within a second or two look like the tissue surrounding it. If it is slow or if the gums seem excessively pink, you may want to call the veterinarian.

Basic Cat Care

Much of the same things that are important for caring for dogs are important for cats. Be sure you know exactly what the cat normally eat, and where she is fed. If there is a dog in the house, too, you will probably need to be sure to keep the cat's food dish up out of reach of the dog. The cat may typically drink out of the dog's water bowl, but it would be best to leave the cat her own water dish.

Beware!

If you are a pregnant woman with a pet sitting business, you need to stay away from cat litter boxes. Cat feces can transfer the parasite causing toxoplasmosis, which can harm the fetus if contracted by a pregnant woman. You will want to find a subcontractor for jobs with cats or simply refuse jobs that entail cat care until you have delivered your baby and are back to work.

Cat Restraint

Cats can be much less tractable than most dogs. Of course, there are always exceptions. And cats that you might assume would give you a lot of trouble sometimes stay rock still while being examined—presumably they think that if they just cooperate, they won't be hurt!

One simple way to thoroughly restrain a cat is with a thick towel (a good reason to keep a thick towel in your vehicle supplies). Make sure all four legs and feet are thoroughly wrapped. Hold the animal snugly enough that he can't get away but not so

From Pet to You

There are several infectious diseases that are transferable from dogs and cats to humans. These are called "zoonoses." You should know what they are and their basic signs.

○ *Cat Scratch Disease*. This disease is contracted through a skin-penetrating bite or scratch from a cat. It can cause flu-like symptoms in general and/or mild to severe swelling at the bite site. Recovery typically occurs without treatment, although antibiotics are sometimes required.

○ *Orf*. Orf is a herpes-like virus that causes skin lesions. It is contracted from direct contact with infected goats and sheep, who show signs all around their mouth and nose areas. Orf typically goes away on its own and if symptoms are mild to severe. If you end up caring for animals with orf (also called "cold sores"), use gloves and try not to handle the animals. Orf is very contagious.

○ *Rabies*. This viral infection affects the central nervous system and is deadly. You should require that all dogs and cats you care for be vaccinated for rabies. And you should get vaccinated as well. If you are bitten or scratched by a dog or cat, there is a definite protocol. If the animal has an up-to-date vaccination record, then the animal has been revaccinated and things should be fine. If the animal is not vaccinated, then it needs to be quarantined and perhaps euthanized, depending on state regulations.

○ *Toxoplasmosis*. This parasite, as mentioned in the sidebar on pregnant women on page 89, is passed from cat feces (a good example of why it is important to keep your hands washed after handling animals and cleaning litter boxes, etc.) and can cause mononeucleosis-like symptoms.

snugly as to encourage him to want to struggle. Some cats can simply be held in place by the scruff of the neck—four feet on the floor or table please! A lot of how you choose to restrain a cat depends on what you need to do and how much the cat is accustomed to being handled.

Although wearing thick gloves seems sensible, they are usually not very effective—ones that are thick enough to fend off a cat bite often are so awkward you can't do what you need to do.

The key is to use the appropriate level of restraint you think you might need—too much might panic the animal, too little isn't effective enough.

Basic First Aid

The two most important things you can do when it comes to first aid for pets under your care are to

1. Have veterinarian's numbers on hand, including the numbers of the pet's regular veterinarian and the closest off-hours emergency clinic.
2. Take a pet first aid class from the Red Cross or anywhere that gives one locally. At least spend some time with a veterinarian or vet tech to learn some basic first aid.

Signs of Illness

The key signs of illness in most pets are lack of appetite, vomiting, diarrhea, or lethargy. If the pet normally greets you enthusiastically at the door, you should be suspicious if she doesn't. When you call the veterinarian, it is helpful to have taken the pet's vital signs, even though they will retake them the minute they have the pet in the exam room.

First Aid Kit

The following items will run you around $50–$75 depending on how much you buy and what level of container you choose to store it all in.

- ○ Stethoscope
- ○ Digital thermometer
- ○ Lubricant
- ○ Alcohol
- ○ Cotton swabs
- ○ Tape
- ○ Latex gloves
- ○ Scissors
- ○ Tweezers
- ○ Antibiotic ointment

Look around to see if there is any evidence that the pet ate something—a loaf of bread or some other item off the counter, or if there is a wrapping or remnants of a plastic item or anything that would indicate the animal (typically a dog) is suffering from some foreign object in his stomach or is ill from overeating or eating something that is not good for it.

If the dog vomited or had diarrhea but is otherwise acting normally—attentive, interested in playing, eating normally—then it may be an isolated incident. Still, take vital signs. If they are normal, then you can probably leave the dog for the day or night with confidence. If you are still concerned even though the dog is now acting normally, come a little early for the end-of-day visit in case you then feel a trip to the veterinarian might be in order—you'll save your client an emergency call if you can get the pet there while the clinic is still open. Or you may want to stop back for an extra visit to check on the pet. You will need to be sure your fee schedule lists what such an extra visit will cost the pet owner, just so they will be prepared. And you will want to have called the owner to talk over the pet's condition with him.

Similar considerations should be taken for cats. The key is whether or not the animal is now acting normally even though it had an accident on the floor.

Wound Care

Another first aid situation you may come across is wound care—a cut from broken glass or any other number of problems dogs are capable of getting themselves into, especially if you let them out or they stay out for the day.

The first thing you want to do is stop or the slow bleeding and determine if the wound will need stitches. Dogs commonly cut their pads and these cuts can be very deep; they often don't require stitches, but they need to be cleaned and wrapped.

> **Tip...**
>
> ### Smart Tip
> Unless a pet is being starved, otherwise shows obvious nutritional neglect, or you are specifically asked for advice, the food choices the owner makes for the pet are not your business; your business is to feed it to her. Most owners who are responsible enough to hire a pet sitter are also bringing their pets for regular veterinary checkups (something you should require anyway to be sure they are vaccinated), so let the client's veterinarian take care of that aspect of client education.

Both dogs and cats are not really happy about having bandages—there is almost no place on their bodies that you can put a bandage that they won't work at tearing it off.

Puncture wounds are the ones to watch out for. If the pet gets a puncture-type wound (as opposed to a slice-like cut) it is best to have the veterinarian check it out. Puncture wounds close up on the surface, leaving a breeding ground for all sorts of bacteria from the cause of the puncture. Puncture wounds demand careful cleaning that is best left to the veterinarian and may require prophylactic antibiotic injections or tetanus follow-up vaccinations.

Client Attitude

Spend a little time in the initial interview talking with your clients about their own attitudes about veterinary care for their pets. Some people are more hands-on and take care of lots of things themselves—if they feel confident in your skills, they are probably going to be fine with you caring for a relatively minor wound and not expect you to run their pet to the veterinarian's office for every little thing. Some people are very neurotic and bring their pet to the veterinarian for every little cut, scrape, runny nose, or hangnail.

You definitely don't want to be shy about getting the pet to a professional for something that concerns you—the pet is your responsibility, after all. But you will become more and more familiar with your clients, and more experienced yourself, and will find that these decisions become easier to make.

Client Profile Worksheet

Date of initial contact: _____

Name: _____

Address: _____

City/state/zip: _____

Directions: _____

_____

_____

Contact Information

Home: _____

Work 1: _____

Work 2: _____

Cell 1: _____

Cell 2: _____

Fax number: _____

E-mail address: _____

Local contact: _____

Contact info for current trip: _____

Most Common Reason for Service

___business travel

___vacation

___weekday lunch visit

___"emergency" visits (client unexpectedly called away)

Pets	Type	Size	Age
Pet 1			
Pet 2			
Pet 3			
Pet 4			

(see other side for additional pets)

Do any pets have special medical needs? _____

_____

Do any pets require special handling? _____

_____

Pet Profile Worksheet

Update this sheet with every job, do one profile for every pet the client has and staple sheets together.

Pet name: _____

Owner name/address: _____

Type of animal: _____ Age: _____

Feeding

What brand and type of food does the pet eat? _____

Where is the pet's food typically purchased? _____

Feeding Instructions

___Dry food and canned food mixed together

___Dry food and canned food fed in separate dishes

___Water in dry food

___Pet tends to eat food immediately and completely

___Pet tends to eat food over course of time

___Pet is a fussy eater

Does the pet get treats regularly? _____

Does the pet have any dietary constraints? _____

(e.g., trying to lose weight, uses prescription-only foods, must have supplements)

Medications

Does the pet receive any medication? _____

What is the medication? _____

What is it for? _____

_____

Where is medication kept? _____

How frequently is it administered? _____

How is it administered? _____

What is the source of the medication? _____

(veterinarian or regular drugstore)

Behavior

Does the pet have any behavioral idiosyncracies? _____

_____

Pet Profile Worksheet, continued

Behavior, continued

Does the pet get along with all other pets in the household? _____

_____

Should the pet be separated from another pet when left alone? _____

_____

Is the pet well socialized with other pets of its species? _____

_____

Exercise

What kind of regular exercise should the pet receive during the pet sitting period? _____

_____

_____

Attach Photo Here

(update photo annually, more often if pet is juvenile)

Service Contract

This agreement is made this_____day of _____ between _____ (hereinafter "Handler"), and_____(hereinafter "Owner")

1. **Purpose of Agreement.** The purpose of this agreement is to state the duties and obligations of the Handler and Owner, respectively, concerning the care and handling of the below described dog(s), horse(s), cat(s).

   Handler: _____

   _____

   _____

   Owner name: _____

   Address: _____

   Phone: _____

   Work phone: _____

   Cell phone: _____

   E-mail: _____

2. **Subject of Agreement.** The animals, which are the subject of this agreement are fully described below. The Owner hereby affirms that the information provided is true and correct, and agrees to indemnify and hold harmless Handler for any damages that may result to the animals, to Handler, to Owner, or to third parties from inaccurate information being provided herein:

   Information about The Animal(s)

   Breed: _____

   Color: _____

   Sex: _____

   Name: _____

   Date of birth: _____

   (Use separated pages for multiple animals)

   The above-described animals are referred to herein as "The Animals."

   Health Information about The Animal(s)

   Chronic illnesses: _____

   Date of last rabies vaccine: _____

   Name, address, and phone number of veterinarian: _____

   _____

   _____

Service Contract, continued

Behavior Information about The Animals

Describe fully previous displays of aggression of ANY TYPE (including aggression toward other animals or people): _____

_____

_____

Authorization. Owner hereby authorizes and empowers Handler to walk/exercise The Animals in the designated locations and public areas, enter the home, and feed the animals.

Indemnification and Hold Harmless. Owner hereby agrees to indemnify and hold harmless Handler, or Handler's duly authorized agent, from any and all liability that may result from the following: any injuries inflicted by The Animals on other animals, on Handler, on Owner, or on third parties; any injuries that may be suffered by The Animals; destructive behavior in the house/house soiling. (Valuables and sentimental items should be safely stored.)

Emergencies. In the event that emergency medical care is necessary for The Animals, it is agreed that Handler will obtain such treatment from any licensed veterinarian, the expense of which will be reimbursed by Owner within two business days.

Emergency contact numbers: _____

_____

Relatives or other contact person (if you can not be reached): _____

_____

Cleaning procedure/solutions. Owner must choose and leave the appropriate carpet cleaner for the Handler. Food dyes and natural pet body fluids can bleach and stain carpeting and are beyond the Handler's control.

Keys.* Owner must provide two sets of keys, one for Handler to carry and one to leave at Handler's home. Owner has checked that all keys work. Keys are not to be left hidden outside by Owner or Handler.

Owner signature: _____ Date: _____

Print name: _____

Handler signature: _____ Date: _____

Print name: _____

Contact number where owner will be: _____

*Who else has a key to your house? _____

Courtesy Amy Carlson, Amy's Animal Care

Emergency Notification Regarding My Pets

In Case of an Accident or Death

In the event that I am incapacitated and unable to make my wishes known regarding my pets while I am away and they are under someone else's care, please honor the following requests: The welfare of my pets are a primary consideration. DO NOT turn over to Animal Control.

Contact the following as soon as possible: _____

Day number: _____ Night number: _____

If they cannot be reached, please contact: _____

Day number: _____ Night number: _____

All expenses for the pets will be guaranteed by them.

If the pets are not injured, they are to be cared for by the nearest reputable boarding kennel, and be kept in the best possible manner until arrangements can be made to get them home.

If the pets are injured, they are to be cared for by the nearest reputable veterinarian. I prefer that my veterinarian be contacted regarding decisions on the pet's care and treatment. They have all of my pet's medical records available and know my wishes.

Contact my veterinarian: _____

Day number: _____ Night number: _____

Contact my pet sitter: _____

Day number: _____ Night number: _____

My pet sitter has the information and authority to care for my pets, and knows who to turn them over to. My pets can be released to my pet sitter from any authorities. _____ Initial

If any pet is injured beyond all hope of recovery, that pet is to be humanely euthanized. _____ Initial

Photographs and descriptions of the pets are attached. For identification purposes these pets are tagged or tattooed with an identifying number or have had a microchip ID implant. _____

_____

Emergency Notification Regarding My Pets, continued

Owner signature: _____ Date: _____

Name: _____

Address: _____

Home phone: _____ Work phone: _____

Spouse/significant other: _____

Parents: _____

My pet's guardian: _____ Phone: _____

Courtesy Amy Carlson, Amy's Animal Care

Other Common
House Pets

There are many pets besides dogs and cats that you may encounter in your pet sitting adventures. Some of the more common ones are covered in this chapter. You will typically not be hired to care for just these pets—unless a client has an entire aviary of finches. Most of them will be animals you care for along with the family dog or cat.

▲

The key to pet sitting for any animal that you are not familiar with is to be sure the owner tells you everything she knows about caring for the animal on a daily basis. Of course, you don't need to know every detail about the breed or every aspect of medical care—you hope you won't need to deal with these things!

What you do need are clear instructions, preferably written, on the following:

> **Smart Tip** Tip...
>
> Be sure when you take on a type of animal new to you that the owner leaves you with a book, magazine collection, Web site, or other resource that he uses himself when he needs to find out more information about something regarding his pet.

- *Feeding.* What kind of food the animal eats, how much, how often, what dishes are used, where it is kept, and where it is bought.

- *Cleaning cages.* You need to know how often, what to use to clean the cage, what to use for bedding material, what to do with the pet while you are cleaning the cage.

- *Exercise.* Are you expected to provide the pet with exercise time outside what the pet gets in the cage it stays in most of the time? You need to know how long the sessions should be and how vigorous.

- *Signs of illness.* You will not be able to learn every detail about every animal's possible maladies, but do have the owner tell you about the ones that are most common and would be the most likely ones to show up if anything goes wrong while under your care.

No Free Lunch

If you take on a new client who has any (or, imagine, all!) of these other house pets in the mix, you need to set a fee schedule to tack on to your basic dog care fee. Don't get lured into thinking that these little critters won't take up much extra time. That can be true, but it also can be true that some of them are a bit fussy to care for and the risks of something happening to them are higher than for your typical cat and dog.

Adding a $5 fee per day or even per visit for each "extra" pet is legitimate and can help you avoid building up any resentment that you need to fuss with these extra animals each time you visit.

Although any good pet sitter will take the utmost care of any animal entrusted to her, you need to also remember that you are running a business. The extra ten minutes per visit that it takes to check in on the cage of hamsters, fill food dishes, water, and even clean the cage is ten minutes that could be spent driving to your next job.

Saying No

There may be some animals that you do not wish to care for. You may even be allergic to some pets. Make sure it is perfectly clear in your marketing literature what animals you absolutely will not take on. If a client still wants you to care for their dogs and cats, perhaps they can get their neighbor or relative to take the cage of chameleons or cockroaches or whatever people dream up to keep as pets to their house. Some of these smaller animals are better kept somewhere where someone is around most of the time anyway.

The key is to be clear with potential clients. Don't be wishy-washy and find yourself caring for animals you don't want to care for. On the other hand, if you are going into the pet sitting biz, you may just need to prepare yourself for anything.

All the Info

Now let's take a look at the *Merck Veterinary Manual*. This classic veterinary guide is a must for anyone who makes their living dealing with animals in any way. You can access the *Merck Veterinary Manual* online for free at www.merckvetmanual.com. The site is highly searchable and includes thumbnails of all charts and figures, which can be clicked on to see larger images.

The manual can also be ordered as a reference book directly from Merck, at any bookstore either from the shelf or special order, and from online book sites such as amazon.com.

The manual is also available on a CD-ROM, which is fabulously useful if you bring a laptop computer on the road with you, and in a handheld format for your Palm Pilot or other personal data assistant.

Merck is a big name in both human and animal health and is a reliable source of fascinating information. The manual gets as technical as you would possibly want to get but it also has lots of general information such as overviews of categories of animals and introductory material about all kinds of animals that any pet sitter wanting to give high-quality care (which should be all of you!) would find intriguing.

Birds

Parakeets are the most common pet bird you will run across. Other birds include finches, cockatiels, and parrots of different varieties. You may run across more unusual birds as well, but unless you are pet sitting at someone's medieval British castle, you probably won't come upon too many peacocks to care for. Turkeys are not high in the pet statistics either, although chickens could be part of the mix if you are barn sitting (see Chapter 10).

For short-term care, say a day or two, you will probably not need to do anything more than keep the water bottle filled and the feed trays cleaned and full of food. For this, you will need to reach into the cage door. You'll need to know how to make sure the bird doesn't get out in the process. And for some of the larger birds in smaller cages, you'll need to be sure the bird won't bite you! Chances are if it's kept as a pet, it won't, but animals can be funny with strange people. It is best to do this while the owner is still around so the bird can get familiar with you while its owner is still there to help it feel comfortable.

When the bird's owner is away for more than a couple of days, you will need to clean the cage as well as keep food and water dishes full. Have the pet owner show you how to do this. For instance, you'll want to know what they typically do with the bird while they are cleaning her cage.

Some birds enjoy other treats besides commercially prepared bird food. If the owner requests that you feed these treats, be sure the owner buys the food, stores it properly (e.g., refrigerated if necessary), and indicates exactly what food is intended for the bird. Sometimes one type of lettuce may be a special treat, and another kind may make the bird sick!

One of the most important things with birds is temperature control. If it is winter in a cold climate, you will need to be very diligent about checking that the furnace is running and the temperature is at the optimum level for the bird. You will probably need to cover the bird's cage at night with a towel. The owner may also ask you to give the bird some flying time.

Birds of all kinds—finches, parakeets, parrots, mynah birds, cockatiels—can be fascinating to interact with. Once you get accustomed to caring for them, you will probably find them to be among your favorites.

Rodents

Hamsters and guinea pigs are common pets, especially in homes with children; rats and mice are also kept as pets in some homes. Again, they often don't require special care. However, their cages can get pretty smelly pretty fast. Cleaning rodents' cages will be necessary if the pet owner is gone for more than a few days. Don't avoid this. It is not good customer service for your clients to come home refreshed from their vacation to a house that smells like urine.

Hamsters and guinea pigs sleep all day and chew, run on the treadmill, or forage around all night. You will probably never see them function during the times you are there. This makes it difficult to tell if they are OK, but you should be able to see whether or not they ate and drank during the course of the night. If your care is over a long enough period, say a week, then you will also need to take the rodent out of the cage to clean it (the cage, not the rodent!).

The owner should leave plenty of food and treats for the animal. Some people like to give their pet rodents some fresh greens and will have a supply in the refrigerator. Remove uneaten fresh food each day because it can go bad.

Always freshen the pet's water at every visit. In fact, it wouldn't hurt to be sure to leave two tubes of water.

Fish

After hamsters and guinea pigs, fish are probably the most popular pets for kids. You will run across them in your jobs taking care of dogs and cats, although the fish will probably not be the main reason you're hired.

Fish don't require a lot, but they can be fussy when it comes to care. You'll need to know how much to feed them and if you are going to have to clean the tank. The most important thing to find out is what to do if the pump and filter stop working.

You'll want to know what the owner would like you to do if you find a fish floating upside down when you arrive at the home. There are things you can do for fish that seem under the weather—one sign of a sick fish are often simply that it isolates itself from the group. According to the animalnetwork.com Web site, the following things are critical when it comes to fish tanks:

- Excellent water quality
- A balanced diet
- Compatibility among fish in tank
- Low stress level

Overfeeding is a problem because the food that goes uneaten affects the quality of the water. Your care will help to maintain all these factors.

Water is best changed at 10 to 15 percent of the tank once a week so if you are providing long-term care for a client's pets that includes an aquarium, you should plan to provide a partial water change for the tank during your care. Make sure the new water is the same temperature and that you remove the chlorine with products that your client should have on hand.

Marine/saltwater aquariums are even more fussy than fresh water aquariums, so you will want your client to provide you with very specific directions on how to care for the aquarium. If fish really interest you, you should think about getting your own aquarium and becoming experienced in their care. And you can read the many fish/aquarium magazines on the market, such as *Aquarium USA* and *Aquarium Fish*, to name a couple.

Ferrets

Ferrets have become very common pets and are interesting animals. They are friendly and fun loving. They have a few peculiarities that you will want to know about.

Ferrets are meat eaters. Their digestive system works quickly, and because vegetable matter takes longer to digest, they cannot get what they need from a strict vegetarian diet. They can be fussy eaters and ultimately they don't eat much, so many ferret owners buy high-quality food (sometimes cat food) for their ferrets.

Some pet ferrets are allowed the run of the house and have been trained to wear a collar; many owners put a bell on their ferret so they know where it is. While under your care, pet ferrets may be confined to a room or cage, but they will appreciate some kicking around time.

If there are other pets in the household—dogs and cats, especially—you will want to be sure to know how the animals get along and if it is OK for them to roam the house together while you are there.

According to the Web site ferretcentral.org, ferrets are often given hairball remedies like the ones given to cats. Not only do ferrets have problems with hairballs, but they also often eat things like rubber bands and other small items found around the house and the hairball remedy helps them pass those things through their system.

Ferrets are trained to use litter boxes. You will want to know from the owner what kind of litter she uses and what kind the pet prefers. Some litters that are used for cats are

> **Tip...**
>
> **Smart Tip**
>
> According to the *Clinical Handbook for Veterinary Technicians*, the proper way to restrain a ferret is to hold it by the scruff of the neck. You need to support its lower body either with the other hand if you have someone else who can examine the animal or in your lap if you need to examine the animal yourself. The *Handbook* also says that sometimes this technique will cause the ferret to gap its mouth open in a yawn, making it easy to examine the mouth, which can be helpful if you are trying to determine if the ferret has something stuck in his mouth or throat.

not recommended for ferrets because of differences in elimination habits, while others are fine.

Ferrets are very entertaining and inquisitive animals. Although you would probably not be hired just to care for a couple of ferrets, you will probably find them an enjoyable addition to your repertoire as a pet sitter.

Rabbits

Another child pet favorite, rabbits are more often housed inside than perhaps in the past when they were relegated to a small cage in the backyard. Rabbit owners often let their rabbits out for supervised runs around the house on a daily basis. And yes, rabbits will chew on electrical cords or speaker wires or other things that will either hurt them or be a pain to replace or repair. Some rabbit owners have portable pens in the yard for their rabbits to get some fresh air, sunshine, and a little grass. The most dedicated of rabbit owners build elaborate outdoor pens for their pets to have extended outside run-around time. Under your care, however, be sure these excursions are well supervised because rabbits dig, their predators also dig, and portable cages can be easily overturned.

Unfortunately, rabbits seem rather delicate when it comes to health and care. The other thing that frequently happens is that their owners become disinterested after the initial enthusiasm—especially when the rabbit is obtained as a little bunny and probably as a gift—and, therefore, you may find that rabbit care is often an afterthought. And many rabbits do not stay in the household more than a few months before they die, are given away, are given up to a shelter, or unfortunately, set free (not a good thing for a domesticated rabbit; it will not last long, succumbing either to predators or to an inability to care for itself).

Bright Idea

Although it is best not to bring small children along on your pet sitting jobs, sometimes it just cannot be avoided. One of the best ways you can put all but the smallest children to work is simply sitting outside the pen of a rabbit in an outdoor cage and supervising the bunny's outdoor time while you take care of cage cleaning or tending to other animals. Instruct the child to check in with you every few minutes to update you on the animal—this way you can keep tabs on the child, and keep the child vigilant in her job. You can also instruct the child to yell if the rabbit is digging out of the pen. You need to determine the safety of this arrangement, of course—if the home has a swimming pool or is near a busy road or anything else that may endanger the child, this is not a good idea.

Let There Be Light

Lizards especially, but also other reptiles, need a full-spectrum light in their cage during the daytime.

Reptiles

You may never have expected to be caring for a reptile, but there are more than seven million reptiles kept as pets in the United States, so there's a good chance you will run across one or two in your pet sitting business. Some common reptiles that veterinarians see as pets, according to the *Clinical Textbook for Veterinary Technicians* are boa constrictors, pythons, and corn snakes (to name just a few possible pet snakes), different kinds of turtles, and lizards such as bearded dragons, iguanas, chameleons, and various types of geckos.

Reptile owners often do not hire pet sitters just for a snake. You're more likely to care for a reptile in the form of adjunct care to a dog or cat. How do you want to handle these if a potential client calls? It is best to give an upfront "no" if you just can't picture yourself feeding a snake live mice.

Your best source of information about reptile care is the pet owner. You will need to follow the owner's instructions carefully to ensure that the reptile stays stress-free while its owner is away.

Restrain Yourself

You may want to know a little about snake capture and restraint in case Mr. Boa gets loose or you need to get him out of his cage. The owner should be able to teach you (in fact, insist on it). Owners should have tongs, a "snake hook," or pole snare in their collection of snake care items that can capture a snake around the base of the head—although in the case of large, coiling snakes you also need to restrain the tail end!

Barn Animal
Care

Not all pet sitters will have barn animals on their list of pet sitting options, but barn care can be lucrative if you live in the right area.

Most people with barn animals will also have house pets (see also the section on barn cats at the end of this chapter), so these kinds of customers can take quite a lot of time, so you can charge considerably more per visit than for just house pet care.

Livestock Care

Don't solicit barn customers unless you have some experience with livestock. If you don't have experience but would like to get some, there are many ways you can get experience. Like most things, offer your services for free and you can get all the experience you want. For instance, most large horse facilities are in a constant search for cheap help. They frequently exchange riding lessons or riding time for help cleaning stalls and other mundane chores.

Tip...

Smart Tip

Keep a pair of boots in your vehicle that you wear only when you are at other people's barns. Also, always wash your hands before tending to your own animals. That way you can be more confident that you didn't bring home any organisms to your barn crew. You might also extend this courtesy to other people's barns—keep some Betadine in a jug of water in your vehicle to rinse your boots before heading from one job at one barn to another.

If you are in an area where horse care can be one of your offerings, then you will also be able to find large animal veterinarians. Follow one of them around for a couple of days and you will learn a lot about livestock care.

You probably won't find yourself being hired to sit for a large commercial facility, such as a dairy barn. To keep pet sitting as your real business, you'll want to take on only livestock that are referred to as "backyard" animals; i.e., they may technically be livestock, but they are really considered pets by their owners.

Fees

Most pet sitters who include barn care on their menu of services charge a general fee for a visit that would include care of one or two horses. Additional horses are charged per horse. So, for instance, for $25 you provide a list of services for two horses for a morning visit.

For each additional horse, charge a surcharge of, say $5 per horse. If there are other livestock, charge a fee that is fair compensation depending on the amount of work that would be required to care for the animal(s). For example, if there is a pen of three sheep, you might charge an extra $10 to care for the sheep as well but not $10 per sheep.

Another consideration in the colder climates is to charge extra for winter care because this requires additional time-consuming tasks like cracking ice out of buckets, taking blankets on and off horses, and maybe shoveling a path or two.

Time Management Tip

If you have a regular job doing lunchtime care for a horseowning client who commutes to an office for a full-time job, you might occasionally be hired to hold the horse for the farrier or veterinarian. If possible, request that the owner make this appointment for a time near your typical lunch visit so you can combine the two visits.

You should plan to spend at least an hour for the morning barn visit (see below for the kinds of things you will need to do), perhaps more depending on the number of animals. For an extended livestock sitting job, you will also need to make a late afternoon or evening visit, which should be shorter than the morning visit because you will probably need to clean stalls and paddocks only once a day. You may also be asked to come by in the middle of the day and feed some lunch.

Services

The services you provide for barn care may include:
- feed hay and grain.
- freshen water buckets.
- clean stalls.
- put down fresh bedding.
- clean paddocks.
- light grooming.
- turn horses out.
- put on or remove blankets.

Each individual client will have his or her own particular things to add to the list.

Horse clients can be good regular customers for things like stopping by each workday to feed some lunch hay, freshen water, and generally check on things.

These same clients may also want to hire you to be around when the horseshoer (often also called a farrier or blacksmith) comes. Farriers typically prefer to have someone there who can hold the horse's lead rope while they remove shoes, trim feet, and nail on new shoes. This can take as little as 20 minutes for trimming the horse's hooves to as much as 45 minutes to an hour per horse, depending on the complication of the shoeing job.

Weight Lifting

A word of caution when it comes to barn work: lift with your knees. No kidding. There are a lot of things around a barn that have the potential to require heavy lifting: full water buckets lifted to their hooks (tip: lift up a half-full bucket, then fill it with another half-full one), grain bags emptied into larger, mouse- and horse-proof containers, bags of shavings, bales of hay, you name it.

While there are many ways around this—water hoses that reach into stalls, hand trucks, tractors, etc.—many times backyard horse situations are not set up to be incredibly convenient. If you are dealing with one horse, it doesn't make much economic

Beware!
Aged horses (upper twenties and beyond) have sight and hearing loss just like humans do. You need to be sure not to startle them or you may get accidentally kicked!

Horse Handling

You will want to be sure to be experienced handling horses if you are planning to add them to your pet sitting list. However, even if you do have equine experience, you need to get a quick lesson from the horse owner in how her horses are accustomed to being handled. Just because your horses are respectful when you feed or don't crowd you at the gate when you enter the corral doesn't mean other people's horses act the same way around people.

Never underestimate the strength of a half-ton animal like a horse. Even the gentlest of horses can accidentally hurt you. Many horses frighten easily and, as a prey animal, every single horse has self-preservation on the top of his list of concerns. The first instinctive move for a horse feeling like he needs to protect himself is to run—a horse who has been taught to respect humans shouldn't run you over, but in the heat of the moment, the horse may not even register that you are there, so stay out of the line of fire. The horse's second instinct, if he can't run, is to defend himself by kicking with his hind legs, striking with his front legs, or, rarely, charging and baring his teeth.

Hand-feeding horses is never a good idea; even if you feed your own horses treats from your hand, don't do this with other people's horses. In fact, you need to learn from horse owners how they want their horses handled.

sense to spend a couple thousand dollars to dig a trench and put in a water line closer to the one horse.

If heavy lifting doesn't do much for you—or perhaps you even have back problems that require you to avoid heavy lifting at all costs—you may not want to get into barn animal care at all. Even if you are able or don't mind lifting a bale of hay or bucket of water, you might want to require that the barn owner set things up as conveniently as possible for when you are sitting.

Horse Care

Horses have delicate digestive systems that are not suited to their size and a domesticated lifestyle. Some special considerations for feeding horses are as follows:

- Horses need dust-free, mold-free, high-quality hay.
- In order to keep food moving through their digestive system, horses drink ten to fifteen gallons of water each day and need access to fresh, ice-free water at all times.
- Even though horses are large and need to eat 10 to 20 percent of their body weight each day to maintain their body weight, their stomachs are quite small and they need to take in their food in small increments.

Horse Vital Signs

Despite their reputation as high-strung animals, horses have low vital signs compared to most animals. Ranges are as follows:

- Temperature: 99 to 101 degrees Fahrenheit
- Pulse: 30 to 42 beats per minute
- Respiration: 8 to 16 breaths per minute

Bad Signs

The most common thing that you will want to keep an eye on when caring for horses is abdominal pain known as colic. Horses have a very simple digestive system, poorly designed for an animal their size. Any number of things can go wrong to cause a horse to develop abdominal pain. Trying to determine the cause of colic is important, but definitely need to know how to recognize the signs of sickness. Some telltale signs that a colicking horse will exhibit are as follows:

- *Disinterest in food.* If the horse has not finished his breakfast when you show up to feed dinner, this is a suspicious signal.

- *No manure in the stall.* Horses pass a lot of manure in a day, and if there isn't any present, the horse may possibly be suffering from what is called "impaction colic" a sort of mega case of constipation. The impaction itself has a cause, but the resulting abdominal pain is still known as colic.

- *Biting at his sides.* A horse in abdominal stress will frequently turn his head around and bite at his sides or kick at his belly because of the pain involved.

- *Profuse sweating and/or trembling.*

- *Getting up and down or rolling.* Rolling is to be avoided when a horse is suffering from colic. If the horse is impacted, there might be a large amount of food waiting in the stomach to pass through to the blocked intestine. This food causes the stomach to be heavy and can twist around when the horse rolls. Anyone who has taken care of horses knows that "walking the horse" is one of the most common suggestions for colic care, partly to help move the bowels but also to keep the horse from rolling. But don't walk the stressed animal to exhaustion!

The key with any of these signs is to call the client's large-animal veterinarian immediately. The vet will ask about how the horse is acting, so you will want to have any observations to tell her. You should also know how to take vital signs so you can report them to the vet, especially temperature. Don't give pain medication until you get the OK from the vet, it can mask important tips for diagnosis.

Smart Tip

Tip...

It may sometimes be impossible, but it is best if you do not have to bring your own small children with you on your pet sitting jobs. You need to concentrate on what you are doing. This is especially true when you are doing barn care. Barns are innately dangerous places with large animals, heavy objects, and dangerous equipment. That means that you need to be fully aware for your own safety and not be preoccupied with the safety of your child, who will be in danger, too.

Horse First Aid

After learning what to do with a colic case, wound care is probably the main concern you will have with horse first aid. A rule of thumb is that the life-threatening seriousness of the wound is directly related to how close the wound is to the heart.

Leg wounds can be of special concern because the rideability of a horse depends a lot on the condition of his legs. As with all animals, wounds first need to be thoroughly cleansed. Most wounds that do not require veterinary attention probably don't need to be wrapped; in fact, the horse probably won't keep the wrap on very long anyway. The two main types of wounds needing veterinary attention are

1. *puncture wounds.* These need to be thoroughly flushed and probably require a round of antibiotics

2. *Deep and long wounds.* These will likely need to be stitched, although sometimes the ability to stitch the wound depends on where it is located.

Horses are also prone to eye trauma; these can often be self-healing but it is not a bad idea to have a veterinarian check the eye for a scratched cornea or problems that could be permanent.

> ## Fun Fact
>
> Goats and sheep do not have top front teeth. That doesn't mean their bites don't hurt! You still need to be careful if you feed them by hand and it is a good idea not to stick your fingers at their mouths. However, they do not tend to bite to be mean. Goats are curious animals and one way they check things out is with their mouths. Proceed with caution—nothing is sacred, including your hair, your gloves, or that little tag on the back pocket of your jeans.

Sheep and Goats

Next to horses, sheep and goats are probably the most common barn animals you will encounter. Goats are often kept as companion animals for a single horse. Sheep are one of the few backyard farm animals that can be kept as pets but also offer a by-product: wool. Both are fairly sturdy animals and with attention to quality feed and rudimentary shelter, (animal care is called "husbandry" in the livestock world), they thrive with minimal attention.

Goats, however, demand attention. They are curious, entertaining, and sometimes frustrating animals! Contrary to popular belief, goats do not eat everything—however, they will *try* everything just to see if it suits their tastes. Most times it will not, and they move on. But once a goat lands on something that suits her discriminating taste buds, there is no stopping her. This can work in your favor when a loose goat needs to be lured back into her pen. Triscuit® crackers seem to be a favorite, and have the added advantage of attracting the goat's attention with the crinkling inner wrapper. Goats also love apples, raisins, popcorn, and many other salty snacks. There are some things that are poisonous to them—including many landscaping shrubs such as rhododendron and yew—but for the most part, unless starving, goats will not eat much of things that are bad for them.

The goat care you will need to provide as a pet sitter will consist mostly of providing fresh water, hay, and maybe a little bit of grain. Grain is typically fed only to goats that are providing milk. If you sit for a milking doe, you will need to milk her twice a day as near to twelve hours apart as possible. If you've never milked a goat before, be sure to get a couple lessons first!

Most goats are very friendly—too friendly in fact—but you will occasionally run across the feisty goat who is interested in butting you. The barn owner will surely warn you know about such an individual, but chances are goats of that nature are not kept long as pets. Most pet goats are "wethers," which is the name for a neutered male goat or sheep.

Sheep are similar to goats, but they are often more timid. Sheep that have been heavily handled from lambs are quite tame and enjoy the company of people. But even these more tame sheep are often timid around strangers, so don't expect to sit around and cuddle with the sheep.

Sheep and goats are both ruminants—animals that have a four-part stomach that requires them to sit around and regurgitate what they have swallowed and pass it along to the next phase of digestion. The most common problem you run across with ruminants (this group includes cows) is that they get blockages that don't allow them to burp (called "eructating" in polite company) and release the gas buildup that is caused by all that fermentation happening in one of those four stomachs. This problem is very serious and requires immediate veterinary attention.

Goat owners have been known to use the over-the-counter medication called Gas-X on mild cases of bloat, but often this only provides relief depending on the cause of the bloat.

In the summer months, goat and sheep sitting may require a little stall cleaning. However, in the winter months, many goat and sheep owners allow the stalls to build up with dropped hay (both sheep and goats are notorious hay wasters) to add to the warmth of the bedding.

Happy sheep and goats are eating, drinking, contentedly chewing their cuds, or walking around butting each other.

Cows

Most of the pet sitting jobs you get in the barn will probably revolve around horses. However, horse owners may also own a stray cow or two. Some people with acreage raise their own meat animals; few people these days keep a family cow for milk.

Cows may be fed from a different source of hay than the horses, so you need to be sure to learn exactly which hay stack to feed to whom. Neither the digestive nor the respiratory systems of a cow are as sensitive as the horse, so they are often fed lesser-quality hay. Athough it won't hurt the cow to receive the horses' higher-quality hay, it will hurt the farmer's wallet and it can most definitely have a negative effect on the horse if it is fed the lower-quality cow hay.

Cows also are often fed fermented hay and grains called silage, which needs to be kept away from the horse.

The biggest sign you want to watch for that indicates a potentially sick cow is one who is down and doesn't get up for long periods of time. So if you do your barn call in the evening and a cow is lying in a certain corner and it is still there in the morning when you return, you probably need to call the large animal veterinarian.

Other Types of Charges

You may find other barn animals in the mix at a backyard barn, but most of them fall under the categories discussed above. For instance, in the horse category you may also encounter donkeys and mules, as well as minature of any of the equids: horse, donkey, or mule. Although Lilliputian in size, they all end up requiring the same basic care because their digestive systems work the same way.

Llamas and Alpacas

Both llamas and alpacas are members of the camelid genus. Farms with sheep often have a resident llama or two because they are very protective of the sheep flock. Llamas require very little care—they do need hay and fresh water, but they eat a small amount each day.

Llamas have been rumored to spit at things they consider a threat, including people, and they do—but they do need to be provoked or feel threatened to be brought to do this. So don't provoke the llama.

Alpacas are rather expensive creatures and are kept for their hair, which is used by hand spinners, weavers, knitters, and other fiber artists. Alpaca farmers will be sure to give you all the details you need to care for their valuable animals.

Pigs

Pigs in the barn are quite a different situation than the potbellied house pets that are covered in Chapter 11. Pigs, especially sows with young, can be quite aggressive and most barns are set up so you feed and care for the pigs from outside the pen. For defense, pigs either run or bite, and they are equipped with substantial teeth to do so.

Be sure the barn owner leaves you detailed information about the pigs' care (there will probably be more than one). Pigs tend to eat prepared pelleted feed, and backyard pigs will often be fed house scraps. They eat a modest amount of hay, and like all animals, they need fresh water.

Pigs will have shelter and an area to roam in. Pigs like to wallow in mud, because they do not sweat, and mud keeps them cool in the summer. Pigs are normally very clean and tidy. They even tend to create a toilet area in their pen. They are quite smart.

The Importance of Gates

The most critical thing you can do when it comes to giving good barn care is to check, double check, recheck, and check once more just to be sure you have shut and latched gates. Many horse owners have things set up so you can feed and water the horse from outside the corral and you don't have to worry about gates. But if you are doing a longer-term barn sitting job where you have to clean stalls and groom animals, you will be opening and closing gates.

The importance of good gate tending can't be underestimated. Wandering horses are a detriment to everyone—horses running in the streets can be hit by cars, seriously injuring and even killing both the horse and the occupants of the car. Loose horses can make their way to the grain room and kill themselves or cause irreversible illness by eating their way through a bag of grain.

Loose goats can decimate the neighbor's garden in a heartbeat. Sheep and cows don't tend to move around as quickly as goats and horses, but if left loose long enough, they can cause lots of trouble and they may cause damage to property and themselves. Lock those gates and check them twice.

A Word about Barn Cats

Barn care may include tending to the resident barn cats. In warmer weather or temperate climates, this may entail nothing more than making sure the cat dish is full of dry food. In cold climates, always be sure the barn cats have access to water; barn cats get savvy to the fact that they get a dish of warm water at each feeding of the livestock and will show up to drink their fill before the water freezes.

Many times the local stray population is the source for the barn's cats. Many of these strays get quite tame with the people they are accustomed to seeing every day. However, as a relative stranger, you may never see the barn cats when you visit.

If you do, you should be careful not to get too friendly with them. Because of their typical stray status, many barn cats may not be vaccinated simply because they can be difficult to catch!

Make sure the owner tells you what's what with the cats in the barn. You also need to know what his feelings are about veterinary care for the barn cats. If you do find that a resident barn cat seems ill, you can attempt to lure it into a crate and tote it off to the veterinarian, but the chances that you can do that—or even that you will ever see the barn cat, especially if it is sick—are slim.

Jungle Fever

Dogs and cats will be the most common pets that you will be hired to care for. However, people are keeping a huge range of animals as pets these days. Sometimes, your dog and cat clients will also have other pets that come as part of the package, so it doesn't hurt to decide ahead of time what you will do if these animals come up when a new client calls. If you do decide that you will take on exotic animals, you'll need to know a little bit about them.

We'll talk about some of the more exotic pets you may come across, but first you need to consider one more thing.

Wild Animals

In most states it is illegal to keep a "wild" animal as a pet unless you have been licensed by the state to do so. Wild animals include raccoons, skunks, foxes, and even fowl such as ducks and geese.

Most states have several wild animal rehabilitation facilities where people can bring animals that they find hurt or seemingly abandoned. (Most young animals that "seem" abandoned are not at all, their mother or father is off hunting or lurking nearby. Wild animals should only be determined to be abandoned if their parent was seen dead.)

If you are asked to care for a wild animal as part of your pet sitting responsibilities, it is best to say no. If the person is licensed to care for such animals, they would not ask you to take care of the animal anyway, as they would want the care provided by an experienced wildlife person.

That being said, there are still several animals kept legally as pets that could be placed in the category of "exotic."

Chinchillas

Chinchillas have been the subject of various fads, so you may run across them from time to time. They have some idiosyncracies that are worth noting.

Illegal Eagles

Some exotics are illegal; such as any animal that is on the endangered species list. This will not come up very often, so you don't need to familiarize yourself with every single possible exotic pet that may be lurking in homes across the nation, but when you do come across something unfamiliar to you, do a little checking. This doesn't mean you have to turn your client in—that is up to you—but you certainly do not want to agree to take care of an animal that is illegal to own.

First of all, chinchillas have a sensitive digestive system. They are typically fed pellets made especially for chinchillas. High-quality alfalfa or timothy hay is also an important part of their diet. It is also recommended that chinchillas be given bottled water as they are very sensitive to giardia, a common parasite in water.

You pick up a chinchilla by the base of its tail because they have a startling defense mechanism of slipping out of their fur! (It grows back.) They enjoy being rubbed and scratched around the head. Because their fur is full of lanolin, chinchillas also require a regular dust bath; pet stores actually sell something called "chinchilla dust," which you put in a container and let them roll around in.

Chinchillas are nocturnal. They like an ambient temperature of around 65 to 75 degrees Fahrenheit, and under excellent care they can live from 15 to 30 years! Check out chin.buffnet.net for lots of information and links to other chinchilla sites.

Sugar Gliders

These unusual pets are popular among a small number of people. They resemble small flying squirrels, require quite a lot of attention and care, and do best in groups. Because they require lots of attention and companionship and develop strong bonds with their owners, many sugar glider owners may never have pet sitters care for them.

Sugar gliders urinate everywhere, so their cages need constant cleaning. Their food needs are very specific, you will need to get detailed instructions from the owner and be sure everything you need is in the house. They do bite if handled, but reportedly not hard enough to break the skin.

If you run across a sugar glider in your client list, check out the Web site www.sugarglider.net for lots of information.

Pet Insurance

Although more likely to be taken out on dogs and cats, owners can get pet health insurance on exotics as well. Be sure to have a question on your client profile sheet that includes whether or not they have pet insurance on their pet(s).

Hedgehogs

These days, hedgehogs are fairly popular. As with most exotics, pet stores carry food specifically for hedgehogs. Obesity is an issue with these spiny little creatures, so it's important they are not overfed.

To pick up a hedgehog, scoop it up from the side so you are picking it up by its soft underbelly. Hedgehogs will curl up in a ball as a defense mechanism, but you can coax them out by rubbing their back spines in a circular motion.

Hedgehogs need their cages cleaned about once a week. They are neat and can be trained to use a litter box in one corner of the cage. Their food and water containers should be cleaned and disinfected regularly, too. Like many small animals, they like an ambient temperature of between 70 and 80 degrees. Hedgehogs are susceptible to cancer, tumors, and something called "wobbly hedgehog syndrome," which is exhibited by running laps in their cage or falling over.

Potbellied Pigs

Now we are bordering on farm animals. However, potbellied pigs are popular house pets and aren't really that exotic. They are typically friendly and clean, and can even be housebroken. Their owners will tell you exactly how to care for them. And veterinarians are prepared to treat them as well, small-animal veterinary practices have seen more and more pet pigs over the years.

Pigs in general are very difficult to handle, but potbellied pig pets are typically very friendly and entertaining! If you are asked to sit for one, be sure it has been leash trained and housebroken.

The most common complaint about pigs is that they are, well, pigs, and are always on the hunt for food. This means you need to be careful about leaving food around and follow all of the owners instructions, which may include locking the refrigerator.

Also be sure that any pet pig you sit for has been taught to respect humans—pigs, like many animals, seek to be dominant and without appropriate training can become aggressive.

Being potbellied, there is nothing small about these animals—the type of pigs kept as pets often reach upwards of 125 pounds!

Pet pigs need lots of exercise and stimulation or they get bored and a bit unruly—a good reason many of them end up abandoned to shelters.

If you find you need to know more about potbellied pigs, check out the Web site of the North American Potbellied Pig Association (NAPPA) at www.petpigs.com.

Monkeys

What kid doesn't think that having a monkey as a pet would be just about the coolest thing? Keeping monkeys as pets is not a responsibility to take lightly. A Web site from the University of Wisconsin (www.primate.wisc.edu) makes a prominent statement against keeping primates as pets, including the fact that they need very specific care and that they are able to transmit diseases from humans as well as contract diseases from humans (such as TB and herpes-B).

If you do agree to tend to a primate, be sure the owner is conscientious. The monkey needs an annual physical and a TB vaccination, at least. Some states and localities require licenses to own an exotic pet like a monkey, especially with species that can transmit human diseases.

The owners will let you know what they are providing the monkey for a nutritious diet. Commercially prepared foods are available. And yes, monkeys love bananas but they need a diverse, balanced diet, just like humans.

Monkeys need lots of exercise and entertainment, so free time is important. They also need a cage, and one that is secure enough to contain a monkey can be expensive. Many owners also put diapers on pet monkeys, otherwise the house will get soiled.

And, yes, monkeys can be aggressive, and dangerously so. If you choose to care for one in your pet sitting responsibilities, it is probably best if the monkey can be left in his cage because they often bond with their human caretakers but are concerned about strangers.

Ultimately, monkeys are wild animals and probably are best left to the care of a person with lots of experience caring for monkeys. The Web site www.monkeymaddness.com outlines a lot of the complications involved in caring for a pet monkey.

Decide Up Front

When you open your pet sitting business, decide ahead of time whether there are certain pets you will not provide pet sitting for. You can always change your mind as you gain more experience and knowledge, but it is best to know what you want your business to be like ahead of time. There's little chance that if you decide you simply do not to care for, for instance, monkeys that your business will be damaged by that!

Wallabies

Unless you are pet sitting in Australia, you probably won't run across a wallaby. But who knows! Like kangaroos, wallabies are a member of the marsupial family. They have pouches and large hind feet and legs like a kangaroo, but they're minature in scale compared to kangaroos. The largest of the species reach around two and half feet tall and weigh around 50 pounds—comparable to a medium-sized dog.

Most people who keep a wallaby as a pet have an outdoor cage for the animal—they do like to graze—and bring them in the house only when they are around and can pay attention to the animal.

Wallabies are subject to stress-related illness and death, so as a pet sitter, anything you can do to help them maintain their normal day will be good. They are quite adaptable to temperature and weather changes, but like any outdoor animal, they need access to appropriate shelter from rain or cold wind.

Pet wallabies tend to be ones that were hand raised with a bottle, so they can be very friendly toward people.

Internet Tip

If you do a lot of research on the Internet, you've probably heard it before, but it bears repeating: be wary of the source of the Web site information. Large, well-known companies can offer more credible information than small fly-by-night outfits. This means that sites like Merck, the ASPCA, and other national animal-related organizations are the best places to look for highly reliable information.

However, that doesn't rule out other valuable sources of Internet info—individual pet owner sites and chat rooms or newsgroups whose topic is one type of pet. You can gain a lot of information from these kinds of sites. You just need to keep in mind that the information can be full of technical errors, like people who talk about a specific drug name but get it wrong or who offer general information about a particular animal based on their experience with one individual they have as a pet.

Use all sources, but use them wisely. Always keep in mind that with pet sitting, you are caring for someone else's pet, not your own, and you can't take chances. You will need to make decisions with the pet owner in mind, not just the way you would do things.

Marketing Specialized Knowledge

After taking care of a few exotic pets, you may end up enjoying them for their unusualness. If you become knowledgeable enough, you could develop quite a specialty business.

However, as with any specialty, your service is needed by few customers within the general population. While you could have a thriving part-time pet sitting business without leaving your high-intensity suburban development, in order to specialize in exotics, you will need to cast your net considerably wider.

This means longer travel times to get to customers. It probably means providing longer visits as well. All of this means more gas for your vehicle and more time spent on one client, which all boils down to the fact that you must ask for higher fees to care for these pets.

In order to command higher fees, it is important to become very knowledgeable about the exotic pets you market yourself to care for. Find out which veterinarians in your area care for which exotic pets regularly. Bookmark the dozens of Web sites that discuss exotics. If your clients' animals are healthy and well-adjusted, then your clients themselves are one of your best sources of information.

Then imagine the cocktail party anecdotes you'll have!

Expanding Your Business

You can grow only so much by adding new clients. Once you add more clients than you can possibly handle yourself, you will need to hire some help. Once you hire someone and add enough clients to keep you both busy, you will need to hire another person, and so on. At some point in your business, you will want to expand your services instead of adding even more clients. Or maybe you want to continue to add more clients but also expand your services.

There are many possibilities for services for pet owners. People are spending more than $6 billion a year in the United States on pet care. Each year it seems that pet owners are willing to spend more and more on their pets' health and well-being.

One of the simplest ways you can expand your services is to expand the kind of pets you care for. Perhaps you have built your business on dogs and cats but see a whole market of horse owners who would appreciate a pet sitter's services. Or if you aren't in a rural area where horse ownership is common, you might consider expanding to birds or ferrets or reptiles or even exotic pets, all of which we have discussed in earlier chapters.

Some Questions

You need to ask some key questions to determine whether to expand your business in a certain direction:

- What will it cost in time?
- What will it cost in money?
- What will it bring to the business in terms of increased revenue?
- What will it bring to the business in terms of increased market?

Each one of these questions needs to be considered in relation to the others.

Pet Specialist

One way you will probably get experience with other pets is when you have a client who has a pet iguana in addition to her dog and two cats who you care for. Or you might have a client who has a dog and a tank full of fish. Whether or not you choose to market your abilities with unusual pets is up to you, but it can be a sideline to your existing business. Word travels fast among owners of large snakes or exotics.

Expanding Revenue, Not Customers

Although the most common type of expansion for any business, including a service business, is to take on more customers, there are other ways of expanding as well. But how does a business make more money without increasing the number of customers? One simple way is to increase the fee for your services, something that is probably inevitable in any service business at some point. We will get to that in a minute.

You can also expand your business and increase your revenue by getting each of your existing customers to spend more. Of course, you need to offer more (no free lunch, remember?), and you will need to weigh the cost of having more for your existing customers to buy with the cost of simply doing the same thing you already do for more customers than you currently have.

More Services

One way to get your existing customers to spend more money with your business is to offer more services than you currently provide. First, you need to look at your menu of services and figure out what you are not currently providing—dog walking, grooming, taxi service to veterinary and grooming appointments, obedience training, show training, and competition training are just a few of the possibilities.

The good news about most of that list, and about a lot of services, is that there is little in the way of additional costs per service. Typically the cost is in time, and perhaps a few supplies. The real costs are in obtaining your own education and then any additional equipment you need to provide the service.

Obviously, adding dog walking to your services doesn't cost anything in the way of supplies. Adding grooming will take both education on your part as well as some equipment expenditures like clippers, a grooming table, some shampooing products, and a dryer.

The same goes for training, whether it's simple obedience or show or competitive training. Depending on how far into it you want to go, you can get away with buying practically no supplies to creating an agility course in your backyard.

All these things are additional services you can offer to your current customer base. They probably won't all want to avail themselves of your new services, but some will. And *voila*! You've expanded.

Products

The other way that you can expand is to be a reseller of products that your existing customers might need. Many pet-related service providers find a product that they really like and use on their own animals and become a dealer for that product—certain kinds of leashes or collars, shampoo products, nutritional supplements, etc. This can be a great way to sell because your personal enthusiasm for the product comes across in a sincere way.

Or you may find that your customers use some everyday products that you could sell to them. This makes their lives a little easier, and makes you some profit. Nutritional supplements, over-the-counter products like flea preparations, and even a brand of pet food.

There are a few disadvantages associated with selling products, however.

- Products have an upfront costs associated with them. Many companies require their dealers to buy a certain quantity each month to keep their dealership status and to get the discount that you need to make a profit on the item.

- You need to have room to warehouse your supplies. With food, this warehousing can be very specific in terms of rodent-proofing.

- Pet owners are accustomed to having a huge array of choices when it comes to pet food, both dry and canned, as well as treats and even leashes, dishes, and other paraphernalia. You probably can't satisfy the pet owner's need for this diversity.

Expanding on Site

Perhaps instead of expanding your service business on the road, you would like to open a grooming shop where dog owners bring their dogs to you. This is a whole different can of worms.

Some Considerations

First, you will need to decide how this can fit in with your established pet sitting business. Can you be around enough to really have a shop of this kind? Or do you plan to hire someone to handle that aspect of the business for you? Hiring an experienced groomer can be the way to go—you don't have to pay to learn grooming yourself, and you can be ready to go as soon as the shop is—but that means it is a longer road to the revenue expansion you are looking for because that person will need to be paid, of course.

Also, while your residential area may be zoned for a type of business like pet sitting, that doesn't entail much in the way of traffic to your house, and you may not be in a residential area zoned for a retail-type business. This means you need to open a shop somewhere else, which means paying rent or purchasing a commercial space, both of which do not come easily with the money in your change jar.

Not only does a commercial/retail space add expense to your business, but it comes with lots of other headaches including maintenance, cleaning, trash removal and a bunch of little things you may not think of until you are swamped with a to-do list of things that have no relation to animals.

Thinking Outside the Box

Some unusual opportunities exist that relate to pet sitting that could bring in additional revenue.

Smart Tip

Tip...

Always be sure to spend some time actually doing the kinds of services you are thinking of expanding into. Work for a dog groomer, spend a few weeks as a clerk in a pet shop, whatever it takes for you to immerse yourself in the work long enough to get a sense of whether you could stand to add that to your list of services. After all, you went into business for yourself so you could enjoy your work. You don't want to blow that whole concept by taking on something that drives you crazy!

Office Care

Many doctors' waiting rooms, office visitor areas, and even restaurants have fish aquariums in their lobbies to soothe the waiting customer. If you become experienced in aquarium care, you could promote a service doing regular maintenance on office aquariums. You could take this one step further and create a business starting up aquariums for offices that don't currently have one. This could be all inclusive—you could have a menu of offerings of different-sized tanks with different total numbers of fish. And you could offer to keep the aquarium stocked with that number of fish at all times. Aquarium care would probably require a weekly or even twice-weekly visit to the office, but like cleaning services, it could probably be done off hours and not interfere too much with your regular pet sitting customers.

Nightwatch or Off-Hours Feeding

Just because an animal hospital or pet shop is closed does not mean the animals don't need care. If you live in a populated enough area where there are several veterinary offices or pet shops, you could make almost a whole business out of off-hours service.

This service could involve being the regular off-hours caretaker certain days of the week. Or you could provide backup when their regular staff is sick or away.

Care will probably include feeding, cleaning cages, and perhaps providing a bit of exercise to the animals. It will definitely include checking in on each animal and reporting to the appropriate person if any animal seems unwell.

Web Sales

If you do decide to sell pet-related products, one thing you can do to enhance sales is create a Web site. Be sure to advertise your site on all your pet sitting literature.

The site should highlight all your product offerings and provide extensive information—it's the Internet, after all, so there's no reason to hold back on information. Show photos and tell sizes of anything that is size-specific. You should also, of course, make sure to promote your pet sitting services by linking to the Web site you created for your pet sitting business.

The pet sitting Web site is mostly for advertising and information on services. For your expansion site, you will need to accept credit card payment if you want to sell online. Otherwise customers will need to print out an order form and mail or fax their order with a check making the transaction a bit more difficult.

Beware!
While Web sales continue to climb, they are not free of complications. You need to be able to keep your site updated regularly if you want good business out of it—nothing makes a potential customer less inclined to order from your site if it was "last updated" two years ago.

Beware!
Noise is a factor when you board dogs (and maybe cats, too!). Dogs bark. And some dogs bark and bark and bark. Kennels use bark collars and other tools to try to get dogs not to bark, but they often don't work and often owners do not want you to use some of these things. You need to consider the neighbors around your kennel and how you are going to control noise. And you need to consider yourself, too! Can you really stand to be in a building with dogs barking 85 percent of the day?

A Bona Fide Kennel

One of the advantages of pet sitting is that you go to the client's house, take care of the pets, and come home. End of story until the next visit. If you decide to take clients' pets to your own home, you will end up with a boarding kennel.

A potential head-butting concept here is that if you have a successful pet sitting business, you have promoted the idea that pets are most comfortable in their own home when their owners have to be away. So if you establish a kennel, you are then having to make the case to your clients that your kennel is the best place in the world to leave their pets.

You will also need to take into consideration many factors like zoning laws, animal welfare legalities, and other things such as vaccination laws that don't come into play as much when you are pet sitting as you are not mixing a bunch of people's pets up together.

Classes

You may be able to expand your business at least a little by offering classes in pet care, pet first aid, basic obedience training, or other kinds of training. You will need to find a space that will allow classes with pets to be conducted. Teaching can be a fun adjunct to your business, and it can bring in business as well!

Training with or without Pet Owner

Instead of giving classes, you can actually charge to train other people's dogs. And you will want to include some one-on-one work with the owner and the dog together. This can be more low-key, more flexible, and even more lucrative than classes.

Rehab

If you have nursing skills or have any specialization (or want to get it) in physical therapy and other rehabilitation for animals, you could promote it and find you gain a client or two a year. This can be lucrative because it requires specialized knowledge and a lot of care, but you need to know you can find customers who would pay for such a service. Talk with veterinarians about the need for such a service in your area.

Pet Taxi Service

Taxiing people's pets to and from veterinary appointments or grooming appointments can be an adjunct to your existing pet sitting service. You can promote this service even to people who are not your sitting clients, although most pet sitters who do this make it clear that their existing clients and jobs come first.

Other Home-Related Services

Extra services over and above feeding, cleaning cat litter boxes, and letting dogs out will bring in extra money from additional fees, create more of an appeal for your services and, therefore, more customers, and also even be somewhat of a necessity.

Pet owners hiring a pet sitter will be pleased to know that the same person is also willing to bring in the mail, water the plants, turn a few lights on or off, and generally help give the home the appearance of being occupied.

Some of these may be things you will do in the course of pet sitting anyway; others may be above and beyond what you think is viable for services.

Get It in Writing

As you learned in the Chapter 8, you will want to have a written contract with your clients. Even if they are repeat clients, do a new one for every job. If it is an ongoing job (like stopping by every weekday to let the dog out at midday), then renew the contract on a regular basis—monthly, bimonthly, or even seasonally, especially if what you need to do changes between winter or summer.

The contract should outline everything you are expected to do for the client. The core of the contract will cover all the pet-related things, of course, as shown in the sample contract on pages 96–97. In an addendum at the end, add a list of anything else, such as the things that have been mentioned in this chapter as add-ons, that you and your client agree you will do.

Tip...

Smart Tip
Always have your expansion services relate closely enough to your core business to make it logical to use your existing clients for marketing. Otherwise, you are simply starting a whole new business.

Extra Services

Here are the possibilities of what you might be able to or be expected to add on to your services to clients. The clients themselves will come up with things that you won't even be able to imagine, like having lunch with her mother-in-law or picking up his shirts from the drycleaner. Only you can decide to what extent you will go in the way of additional services!

Mail

Bringing in the mail and newspapers can be one of the more common jobs you may be asked to do. Although the post office and newspaper delivery will suspend service for even short periods of time, it can be just one more thing to do if someone is going away for anything less than ten days or so. Providing this service should not be a problem.

You can decide to charge a fee, or you can incorporate this as automatically part of the service you provide. This doesn't mean you don't get paid for the service, but your prices can be a little higher and this kind of add-on can justify it. It's like paying a little extra at the gas pump for full service on a rainy day or paying the fee for using an ATM from a different bank—convenience can be worth the cost, it just depends on the situation.

Plant Care

Plant care can start to get beyond the simple service of picking up the mail on your way up the driveway. If you are willing to care for houseplants, you will want the client to provide very specific instructions on how to do that—how many times to water the plants while they are away, how much to water, whether to rotate the plants for location or sun angle.

This is not an "as you are walking up the driveway" kind of service. It not only requires special attention, but the plants could die under your care! Be sure to follow instructions to a T, and be sure to have a clause in your contract that says that you are not responsible for the plant's death—probably only a serious issue if the plant is a rare orchid that goes for $1,000 and has to be flown in from the Amazon on one particular day of the year, or the pot was a one-of-a-kind that the owner inherited from her great-grandmother and was made in the late 1800s. Of course, if you accidentally knock a plant off a hanger and smash the pot and the plant gets mangled, it would be good customer service to replace the plant (with a high-quality one from the florist, not a spindly one from the department store) and offer to replace or pay for the pot.

Cleaning

Again, housecleaning goes way beyond the scope of pet sitting and other simple, as-you-go tasks. If you are inclined to take on this kind of thing, then it can fit into a pet sitting business quite well. Maybe the owner simply wants someone to freshen up the toilet bowls or wipe the accumulated dust off the counters. But if it is everyday stuff, then the owner will probably need to hire a dedicated house cleaner and not rely on the all-in-one pet sitter!

However, you should plan to clean up any areas that are specifically related to the pets under your care. Litter boxes, food bowls, and water bowls should all be cleaned on your last visit before the owner comes home. You should also plan to do the areas around the litter box and food dishes. Shake pet blankets out and even wash them if they are washable (this may mean either hanging around long enough to wash and dry them or giving the dog a temporary replacement the next to last time you visit in order to take the blankets to wash at your home or a coin laundry). If anything got soiled, be sure to give it special attention. If you are taking care of the pet in the owner's home, the owner should come home to a house that smells as fresh and clean as when the owner is around, and not like a kennel. That's not good for business.

Shopping

Some owners might request you do shopping for them. This may be just shopping for food for the pets because they didn't get the chance to stock up before they left. Or they may actually ask if you would stock up on some basics and perishables for them right before they come home—things like milk, juice, eggs, and some meat and vegetables or a prepared dish for a just-got-home dinner.

Whether you want to add this to your list of services is up for grabs. It may be beyond the scope of what you want to spend your time doing. First, it has nothing to do with pets. And second, you have to make a special trip for this, it is not something in the home that you can do with your regular visit. A grocery store may not be right on your way to the pet owner's house.

If you agree to do this, ask the owner for an approximate amount of money up front to cover the groceries. You shouldn't be using your money to cover these kinds of expenses. And charge a fee that would reasonably compensate you for your time and gas money. And if any purchase requires a trip to some specialty shop, charge a surcharge. If you don't mind offering these services but don't want everyone to ask for them, surcharges will help discourage only those who really find such a service helpful.

Being Around for a Home Maintenance Appointment

Many working homeowners have great difficulty scheduling maintenance appointments because it is hard to be there. This service is similar to pet sitting and can either be an adjunct service to those clients who use you for their pet care or as a separate service that you offer to the world at large.

So, expand away to your heart's content if you need to or want to. Just do it with your eyes open and keep your ears tuned for innovative things to add to your core business.

Appendix
Pet-Sitting Business Resources

Hundreds of books have been written about dogs alone. For every animal you may care for there are dozens more books than what are listed here. However, these are suggestions for a shelf of books that you should have to help you with almost every situation that may arise.

You may find that you prefer a different "owner's" veterinary manual than the ones listed here. Plan to spend some time reviewing the books in a well-stocked bookstore and choose the one that works best for you in how it is set up. However, be sure to check the credibility of the author because you want to make sure the information is accurate.

Books about Animals

Aggression in Dogs, by Brenda Aloff, Dogwise Publishing.

Cat Owner's Home Veterinary Handbook, by Delbert G. Carlson and James M. Giffin, Howell House.

Clown Fishes and Sea Anemones: Everything about Purchase, Care, Nutrition, Maintenance, and Setting Up an Aquarium, by John H. Tullock, Barron's Complete Pet Owner's Manuals.

Dog Owner's Home Veterinary Handbook, by James M. Giffin, M.D., and Lisa D. Carlson, D.V.M., Howell House.

Dr. Pitcairn's Complete Guide to Natural Health for Dogs and Cats, Richard H. Pitcairn, Rodale.

Exotic Animal Medicine for the Veterinary Technician, by Bonnie Ballard, D.V.M., editor, Iowa State University Press.

Horse Owner's Veterinary Handbook, by James M. Giffin, Howell House.

Keeping Livestock Healthy, by N. Bruce Haynes, D.V.M.

Merck Veterinary Manual, by Susan E. Aiello, Asa Mays, and Merck.

Books

Clinical Textbook for Veterinary Technicians, by Dennis M. McCurnin and Joanna M. Bassert.

Marketing Your Business, by Ronald A. Nykiel, Ph.D.

The Everything Home-Based Business Book, by Jack Savage, Adams Media.

Running a One-Person Business, by Clause Whitmyer and Salli Rasberry.

Sit and Grow Rich, by Patricia Doyle, Upstart Publishing.

Small Business Accounting Simplified, by Daniel Sitarz, Attorney-at-Law.

Your First Business Plan, by Joseph Covello and Brian Hazelgren.

Web Sites

Patti Moran's Professional Pet Sitting Products, www.pattimoran.com

Pet Sitter's International: Pet Sitting Excellence Through Education, www.petsit.com

Merck Veterinary Manual, www.merckvetmanual.com

Glossary

Animal husbandry: the caretaking of animals

Better Business Bureau: a consumer watchdog organization that keeps tabs on businesses and their consumer relationships

Bonding: a type of insurance protecting the homeowners from people who perform business services at your home

Capillary refill time: how long it takes the mucous membranes to regain normal pink tones after blanching from pressure

Colic: a stomach ache of any origin and a common and serious ailment in horses

Eructate: belching, in animal care usually referring to the important release of gases generated by ruminants such as cows, sheep, and goats that is generated as their feed breaks down in their digestive system

Exotics: animals kept as pets that are a bit more unusual and often from "exotic"

Farrier: a person who works with iron who is also sometimes a horseshoer

First aid: the immediate critical care given to a wounded or injured animal or person

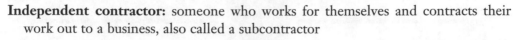
Independent contractor: someone who works for themselves and contracts their work out to a business, also called a subcontractor

Intramuscular: into the muscle, as in a method for administering an injected drug or vaccine.

Kennel: a facility where animals are taken care of for long periods or an individual cage or crate used to contain an animal

Pole snare: a type of restraint used to grab and restrain a snake (see also "snake hook")

Pulse: the number of heartbeats per minute

Rabies: a highly contagious and always-fatal disease of the central nervous system in mammals

Respiration: the number of breaths per minute

Silage: a type of fermented feed usually fed to cows

Snake hook: a type of restraint used to grab and restrain a snake (see also "pole snare")

Subcutaneous: under the skin, as in a method for administering an injected drug or vaccine.

Toxoplasmosis: a disease carried by parasites transferred in cat feces and damaging to an unborn fetus, making it important that pregnant women do not provide cat care.

Vaccines: drugs that help provide immunity to certain diseases

Veterinary technician: a person who has graduated from a program that trains for technical services to veterinarians

Vital signs: signs of life, such as pulse, respiration, and temperature

Zoonosis: a disease that is transferable from animals to humans.

Index